Daniel Curry

Christian Education

five lectures delivered before the Ohio Wesleyan University on the

foundation of Rev. Frederick Merrick

Daniel Curry

Christian Education

five lectures delivered before the Ohio Wesleyan University on the foundation of Rev. Frederick Merrick

ISBN/EAN: 9783337260040

Printed in Europe, USA, Canada, Australia, Japan

Cover: Foto ©Lupo / pixelio.de

More available books at **www.hansebooks.com**

CHRISTIAN EDUCATION

FIVE LECTURES

DELIVERED

BEFORE THE OHIO WESLEYAN UNIVERSITY

ON THE

FOUNDATION OF REV. FREDERICK MERRICK

BY

REV. DANIEL CURRY, LL.D.

FIRST SERIES.

NEW YORK: HUNT & EATON
CINCINNATI: CRANSTON & STOWE
1889

Copyright, 1889, by
HUNT & EATON,
NEW YORK.

INTRODUCTION.

THE lectures embraced in the present volume constitute the first series of an annual course provided for by the liberality of the venerable Rev. Frederick Merrick, ex-president of the Ohio Wesleyan University. After a long life spent in the service of this institution, he has crowned his benefactions by an ample endowment of a foundation for a course of lectures, to be delivered annually in the university, on *Experimental and Practical Religion*. The following extract from the instrument by which he conveys his entire property to the board of trustees for this purpose, explains the character of this foundation:

Extract from the agreement of Frederick Merrick and the Trustees of the Ohio Wesleyan University.

" The said Frederick Merrick, believing that the Christian religion tends, above all else, to the elevation of the human race, and that consequently the usefulness of institutions of learning largely depends upon the influence of religion prevailing among the teachers and pupils, requires, as tending to this end, that said trustees shall appropriate at least six hundred dollars per annum to secure the delivery of a course of, at least, five lectures before the faculty and students of said university upon *Experimental and Practical Religion*, each collegiate year after his, the said Frederick Merrick's death; the lecturer or lecturers to be selected by the faculty of said university as early as the month of January preceding the collegiate year in which the lectures are to be delivered."

The founder of this course of lectures expressly desires that the words which he has adopted to indicate the range of these lectures shall be understood in a broad and comprehensive sense. The term "*Experimental Religion*," thus understood, contemplates the Gospel not only as a hidden power in the soul, molding the personal character of the believer, but as an overt force in the world, shaping and controlling the institutions of men. And the term "*Practical Religion*," expresses the formal application of the doctrines and morals of the Gospel to all the vital issues of the day. Thus understood, the Gospel addresses itself not only to the direction of the outward life of single individuals, but to the solution and regulation of the many complicated questions that spring up in the relations of men with one another. Thus all questions involving the evangelical work of the Church, all social movements of modern civilization, all questions of the rights and obligations of property and of labor, all questions of government, citizenship, and education, all questions of freedom of thought and utterance, in short, all matters touching on the welfare of men, so far as these matters stand related to the Gospel of Christ, come within the proper scope of these discussions.

The lecturers on this foundation have accordingly a wide field before them, including whatever the Christian religion, as a recognized factor, has done, historically, or, by its nature and design, can properly be expected to do, in the world.

The lectures provided for on this foundation were intended to begin only after the founder's death. But as it was his desire that the first course should be delivered by his life-long friend, the Rev. Daniel Curry, D.D., then already well advanced in years, it was so arranged, at the private expense of the founder of the course. The volume before us is the result of this wise forethought. Doctor Curry's sudden death shortly after leaves these lectures almost his last service to the Church.

It is proper to announce here that before this volume has met the public eye, the second course of lectures on this foundation will have been delivered, under the same auspices, by the venerable ex-President McCosh, of Princeton University, and will soon be published in a companion volume.

W. G. WILLIAMS.

Ohio Wesleyan University,
　　DELAWARE, O., *March* 1, 1889.

CHRISTIAN EDUCATION.

I.

CHRISTIAN EDUCATION—INTRODUCTORY AND GENERAL.

THE subject of Christian Education is a very broad one, and it has received the attention of a very great number of learned and judicious writers. We come to it, therefore, without the hope of awakening interest and gaining attention by novel or startling announcements. The importance of the subject will, however, justify the reiteration of its great truths; and the relations to the subject in all its practical conditions of those whom we are to address may be relied upon as a pledge of an interested hearing. The wide extent of the subject, and the abundance of its matter, render necessary a rather broad and therefore general treatment of the matters in hand, which, of course, must exclude any fullness of details which would otherwise be desirable because of their practical utility; even from among the more general features of the subject with which we must deal only a few can be selected for use. Some of these will be given in the successive lectures. But, as a pioneer, the work assigned to the present lecturer is chiefly to prepare the way for those that shall follow; and while it is our high privilege to enjoy a priority in time and sequence in the series of annual discussions of this all-important theme, we must depend on what shall be done by our successors for all that shall make that priority an honorable position. We doubt not, however, that we shall be heard patiently and judged candidly. We ask no more.

Coming to speak in this presence, as we now do at your summons, on the very extensive subject of Christian Education, with which large and fruitful theme we are to be exercised, it may be well to begin with a rapid survey of the situation and its environments. We are met as an association brought together for the one ruling purpose of giving and receiving education. But this general design is here to be ostensibly prosecuted for certain well-ascertained purposes and by definitely-appointed methods. We must, therefore, take due cognizance of the scope of our appointed work and the agencies employed, together with their religious intendments and the ecclesiastical relations in which we stand. Our discussions, and the conclusions to which we may come, must all be in harmony with these conditions, and they must be so ordered as to answer to their requirements.

We shall be concerned with the general subject of education only within the restrictions imposed by these conditions. The subject-matter to be handled must fall within the specific designation Christian, implying that the kind of education now to be considered must be of the Christian type. Standing among the appointments and appliances of this seat of learning, we should also be not unmindful of its paternity and its history, which have determined its purposes and dictated its methods. Our relations to the Church, and to society at large, must enter into the account, and, to some extent, give direction to our discussions.

To receive and to impart instruction is the lifelong occupation of every rational being, and this work is quickened and intensified in proportion as men rise in intellectual and moral power. But, because childhood and youth constitute the specially receptive period of life, young people are usually contemplated as eminently the proper subjects of education. The ancient Greeks called the whole work of education παιδεία, which in various combinations survives in our own language, always retaining its original meaning, and so clearly implying that youth is pre-eminently the time of life in which the processes of education must be chiefly effectuated. By both his mental character and his conditions the child becomes a learner, and his character and career in after life are usually effectually and finally determined by what is learned in his youth. And accordingly, by the provisions of nature, and also by the positive law of God, the simplest and the most sacred of the social institutions is founded on relations that carry with them the opportunities requisite for giving, and the obligations to receive, instruction. The family is the oldest, and always the most sacred, of human associations; it is also greater than any other in its capabilities for good. This, on the human side, becomes by natural stages the tribe and the nation, the State; and on the Godward side it becomes the Church of the living God, "of whom the whole family in heaven and earth is named." In the family the child receives the primary lessons that usually go with him through life, and effectually determine his character and destiny; and to this the work of the school is principally auxiliary and supplementary. So, too, the organic Church springs naturally from the family, in which, indeed, the church life must begin in respect to both its ordinances and its instructions in righteousness. The mind of childhood and youth calls for both intellectual and spiritual instruction, and only by the harmonious blending of these can its development be saved from one-sidedness and deformity; and therefore any properly-ordered system of education must unite these two elements. These thoughts seem to be recognized and emphasized in the things among which we are standing. Their implied requirements should also be practically and effectively regarded.

It is to be presumed that we properly appreciate the demands which our position makes upon us, and that we cheerfully accept the resultant obligations. We are Christians both from convictions and associations; and as educators, our work must be conformed to the requirements of that fact; and if so, the instructions that we give will be positively and distinctively Christian. We are also specifically Methodists—a fact that should not be permitted to lose its significance; and while holding firmly, in common with many others, the great catholic verities of the Gospel, we also emphasize our appreciation of a subjective religious life and experience, to be demonstrated in an earnest evangelistical propagandism. Our form of faith is that of Paul, of Luther, and of Wesley; and of this last, who combined in his own life, and in complete harmony, large intellectual acquirements and a broad and

deep spiritual culture, our institution bears the honored name. It should be our constant concern that all which that name suggests shall be realized and made practically effective among us.

We set out with the concession to ourselves and our profession to the Christian public, that according to our view secular learning constitutes only a part, and that not the most considerable, of a well-rounded education; and we are also well aware that without some good degree of mental training and enrichment, the spiritual development is very likely to be disproportioned, and the religious life neither symmetrical nor wholesome. We do well, therefore, to conjoin the two sides of the common whole in order to raise up a generation of richly-endowed, sturdy, and cultured Christian scholars; devout men of letters, scientists whose open vision will not fail to find the foot-prints and the hand-marks of the Creator in his works, and statesmen who shall guide affairs in righteousness. The world waits to see the coming of such a race, which shall combine the most luxurious growth of both moral and intellectual greatness with the deepest religious experience and the most earnest and active consecration in doing good. Only as they exist and be carried on for the accomplishment of these ends can the action of the Church in founding and maintaining such institutions be justified. Their reason to be is bound up with their earnest purpose to accomplish their specific and much-to-be-desired work.

After such an appreciation of the object to be reached, the next, and scarcely less important qualification of the teacher is a just conception of the needs and the possibilities of the subjects of his instructions and of the character and scope of the lessons to be given to them. The efforts of both teachers and pupils should be steadily directed toward clearly-apprehended ideals, the realization of which should be kept in view and earnestly striven after. These ideals must embody the best style of manhood in character and conduct; and we shall all agree in saying that such a character must be definitely and thoroughly Christian. The conviction must be firmly fixed in our minds and hearts that the business of our Christian institutions of learning, and of our Christian education, is to produce, under the inspiration of the Holy Spirit and the direction of the word of God, well-rounded and matured Christian characters, and by their multiplication to reconstruct society according to the principles of the Gospel. We place before our thought the nascent intellect, with its vacuity of knowledge, but with large potentialities; the germ which, rightly cultivated, will certainly become a large and productive and beautiful plant. This is mind in embryo, which, by its normal unfolding and growth, is to determine the value of the work of instruction. The wise teacher knows that this is to be done, not by a monstrous or disproportionate development of some one faculty, but by the symmetrical education of the whole, and especially with a just recognition of the value of the moral and religious elements of the character and of its native proclivities to evil. Coming thus to his calling with the requisite knowledge of the subject to be wrought upon, and of the means and methods for doing the work, and having a just conception of the end to be accomplished, the teacher, if at all competent to his duties, can scarcely fail in his efforts for the development of noble and worthy characters.

The one and only subject upon which the processes of education are to be performed is the human mind, the rational man, beginning with him in his infantile immaturity. We might speak of the physical man, with his animal life and instincts all tending to completeness; but for that department of our being Nature itself has made the needful provisions, and only asks to be allowed to complete its work with the least possible interference. The care of the body is therefore only secondarily and remotely a part of the work of education. Or, we might delay to consider the physical instincts which belong to man in common with all other animals, and all interference with which tends not to improve, but to pervert or destroy. But of these we need say nothing, since they require no teaching, but only to be let alone. Mind, in the proper sense of that term, can be predicated only of man, of all the denizens of our world; and in the human subject it at first appears only as an unrealized potentiality. But, like every other new-born living thing, it has the instincts of growth, which, among possible conditions, certainly reaches out to the consummation of its tendencies. None of the distinctive characteristics of an intelligent soul—neither intellect, nor taste, nor conscience—can be predicated of the mind of the new-born infant; and yet all these are sure to appear in its normal development, unless it shall be effectually dwarfed and depressed, even to monstrosity, by unfavorable environments. Among suitable conditions the seed invariably becomes a plant "after its kind," and the bud unfolds into foliage and fruit; and so the mind has its ideal possibilities which it instinctively seeks to realize, and which are perfected or spoiled according to its opportunities. Its surroundings become its effective educating agencies, and the subject infallibly attains to knowledge and taste and conscience (the last in both its discriminating and its impulsive qualities) according as it is instructed. And precisely here are the conditions that make education both possible and necessary. The impelling force is the spontaneous struggling of the mind after growth and form; but these tendencies may be quickened or repressed by extraneous causes, or their development may be modified so as to fashion the character after the desired model, for more or less and for better or worse. We are speaking, of course, of tendencies which may or may not be realized, but which will in most cases result in accomplished facts.

To become educated, after some sort or fashion, is the certain destination of every rational being. Even a Casper Hauser, shut up in his dungeon from his birth, and not allowed to see or hear any thing, still gains some notion of the world beyond himself by the senses of touch and taste and smell. But whenever all the senses are permitted to operate freely among suitable conditions, the mind becomes thoroughly awakened to activity, and at length it is stored with ideas. The external world in which he exists is the child's primary school, and, with only the fewest additional aids, also of the untaught savage, with whom the principal conditions of childhood are continued through his whole life-time. In her teachings Nature deals freely in object-lessons, with the appliances for which her school-rooms are abundantly supplied; but without the kindly instructions of the living teacher these are only very partially available. The discoveries of modern science demonstrate nothing else so marvelous as the fact that, in the presence of all the phenomena of the material world, even learned men have lived and died, in long lines of successive generations, without seeming to see them, and, of course, without any notion of their significance. To learn to observe and intelligently interpret the things that confront the senses is itself no inconsiderable item of a practical education; and for this work the helpful offices of the teacher are necessary.

The world is a vast museum crowded with objects that potentially illustrate every part of the science of nature, but until comparatively recently most of the things that now so clearly teach the history and philosophy of the material world were as unintelligible as the pages of a book written in an unknown tongue. The fault was not in the organs of sense, for these appear to be especially keen and active with the child and the savage, but in the defect of instructed and disciplined aptitudes of mind to perceive what is obvious and to interpret Nature's teachings. In natural researches men find what they look for; and they that do not seek will certainly fail to find; and the same rule applies with but slight modifications in matters of metaphysical and spiritual inquiry. This, indeed, is the basis of the parable of the preacher, "The wise man's eyes are in his head, but the fool walketh in darkness." Every one gifted with a normally-constituted physical system has all the apparatus needed for the acquisition of knowledge; is capable of becoming educated; and has decided natural tendencies of mind toward the realization of all these possibilities. The senses themselves need no teaching, but the perceptive faculties, by which the offices of the senses are made available, though naturally obtuse and slow of development, may become acute and of wide range by the aid of instruction and discipline. The mind, in its primary state, is both empty and helpless till aroused by sensations from without, from which many of its first lessons are received; and beyond these very simple things it must be led forward by instruction; and if so guided its possible attainments are practically unlimited.

The wise educator must, therefore, begin with the recognition of the instinctive tendencies of the mind to unfold itself by virtue of its sense-perceptions and of its resultant subjective conceptions. The influence of knowledge upon the mind is directly good and wholesome. It increases the soul's capabilities, affords it healthful exercise, and by supplying food for thought it invigorates its thinking powers. Truth in the mind, of any kind and respecting whatever subject, exercises an elevating influence, and therefore it increases the soul's acquired wealth and also its capabilities for both acquiring and appreciating its own stores. The education that is designed to result in a noble and symmetrical character should not fail to build for itself a broad and deep foundation, made up of all the knowledge of the schools. The alphabet and the conventional value of its letters, the combination of these to form words to serve as vehicles of thought, and these duly freighted and their burdens borne inward and treasured up in the understanding, not only increase its knowledge but develop and enlarge its powers. The intuitions of numbers and quantities, with their combinations and proportions (we call them mathematical axioms, which we can neither prove nor doubt), because, unless carefully studied, they cannot proceed beyond the simplest problems, become means of instruction almost exclusively as the kindly offices of the teacher render them available. Though such merely natural knowledge is not of itself sufficient to fashion the character in its completeness, its certain tendency and the mind's occupation with its processes are favorable to the development of the very best spiritual aspirations. The wise character-builder, whose ideal is the perfection of the soul's possibilities, will begin his work at the foundation, since the lessons of primary instruction precede in both the order of time and of natural sequence all that is comprised in higher education. The true conduct of life consists in the right adjustment of the lower with the higher elements of man's nature, and the latter can be held in its proper supremacy only as it is strengthened and furnished for its work. An empty mind, an uncultured spirit, is comparatively powerless against the animal impulses, and the body can be kept under only as the mind becomes occupied and employed with higher intellectual and spiritual thoughts and exercises.

But both our sense-perceptions and our purely intellectual intuitions reach out in their influences beyond simple logical reality; they tend continually to ally themselves to the æsthetical and the ethical, the sense of beauty and fitness, or their opposites, and of right and wrong in character and conduct. In addition to the logical knowledge that comes to the mind by its perceptions and resultant conceptions there appear also its likes and dislikes, and also ethical approvals and disapprovals. The practical instructor must therefore duly recognize these original elements of mind, since any system of education which fails to accord them their proper consideration must be disastrously defective. The mind is one, and in its furniture no truth stands apart and alone; and in all properly-ordered education there is much more than simply a collection and correlation of facts; but these also extend their influence to and tend to fashion the whole spiritual being. The lessons taught in the schools, even the most abstract and secular, naturally exert a healthful moral influence (unless perverted by other causes) upon the minds of the learners; and only in that fact do we find a justification of the policy that the Church shall become the promoter and patron of secular as well as of sacred learning.

But, before proceeding further, we must return to our former line of thought, which needs to be further pursued and its details elucidated. We have seen that the mind's capacity and appetencies for knowledge are to be responded to by the lessons of instruction. The outward organs supply the required sensations from which proceed the sense-perceptions, and through these the subjective self comes into consciously recognized relations with the objective world. Then the inward thought, the mind acting introspectively, is turned toward its own processes, dealing with what has been received from without, mingled with and modified by its own original suggestions. Thus the soul rises into its appropriate sphere of knowledge, which is broader than the farthest stretch of thought, with power in itself to apprehend and appropriate truth. The objective world is now seen standing over against the subjective self, each another than its alternate. And now Casper Hauser is brought out of his dungeon to look upon the sky and the sunlit earth as something quite apart from himself, and with which he must become acquainted. And from this point his increase of knowledge will be only in degree and form, not in kind. Science is one in its essential nature, though its objects, and therefore its forms, are innumerable; and the pupil that has learned to recognize his own individuality has taken the initial lesson upon which all further learning must be built.

Consulting the mind's reports of its own active states we are introduced to two other spiritual systems in the soul quite distinct from and independent of the domain of the merely logical understanding. In one of these we become aware of certain states of mind which seem to be related to external objects, somewhat in the nature of effects and causes, which give rise to a peculiar form of pleasure and displeasure, of delight and disgust, quite independent of their external and sensible properties. This capability of the spiritual nature, which is clearly original and ultimate, because it wants a name we designate Taste, and describe it as the æsthetical faculty. By this the conscious spirit becomes cognizant of the existence of an element in its own being quite different from the logical understanding, and to which it intuitively assigns a higher place. And since this is an integral element in man's nature it demands appropriate cultivation, in order that the character shall be symmetrically developed; and in proportion to the proficiency attained in these things will the subject of instruction be raised into a higher plane of life and thought, and his capabilities of receiving and imparting pleasure will be increased. The æsthetical faculty properly developed and disciplined opens to the soul's consciousness a new and richly-furnished sphere of existence, without the knowledge of which there cannot be completeness of character.

Of similar characteristics in many particulars, but incomparably more lofty and authoritative, is the ethical element, which manifests itself to the interior consciousness, but which also recognizes its external object; and this it instinctively invests with all the sacred attributes of power and wisdom and essential righteousness; the reproduction of which in the human soul becomes formulated in the ideas of right and wrong, of duty and responsibility. Intellectual truth, when consciously manifested, is freely assented to, and no more than that is required. So, too, the beautiful is recognized and valued, but only for itself and the pleasure that it affords. But the sense of right is also a sense of duty, commanding homage and devotion, and the heart instinctively assents to the claim as the most fitting and the duty imposed as paramount. This faculty—we call it the conscience—dominates the whole man, and asserts its authority over not only the conduct of the life, but also and pre-eminently over the inward spirit and intents of the heart. And as this is among the earliest of the mind's intuitions, and of perpetual force and obligation, it should be assigned no secondary place in the education of every rational soul.

These things suggest what should be the practical work of the educator. He must have some just notion of the capabilities and the wants of the subjects of his teaching, and of the required agencies and methods for doing his work: the fashioning of a character learned, cultivated, and thoroughly conscientious.

Because the beginning of the mind's development is in the sense-perceptions, the quickening and disciplining of the perceptive faculty is a primary necessity in education. No faculty is capable of a greater increase of its powers, and scarcely any other is so much and so generally neglected; for most men go through life with only the scantiest knowledge of the things that lie all about them. The external world is a vast lyceum richly provided with the appliances for instruction; but these become available only as they are applied and their nature and action interpreted by those already initiated into their mysteries. Each one sees in the world the things with which he has come to feel an interest, and accordingly the perceptions are affected by the moods and habits of the observer no less than by his purposed attention, and whatever is perceived enters into the mind and becomes its property and furniture. These considerations intimate to the practical educator what are his work and his opportunities; for as the perceptive faculty is the principal subjective agency by which the mind may be enriched, and because this is especially capable of increase by cultivation, as to both its force and its accuracy, to this should his most careful attention be directed. Here the teacher's own ideal becomes especially effective in determining what shall be the special subjects of thought and study of his pupils, so that his personal enthusiasm may be reproduced among them. Some good degree of learning—the more of it the better—is indispensable for the instructor; but not less so is professional enthusiasm in respect to the work in hand, and relative to both the matter of instruction and in its appreciation by his students. The material world, which seems at first to present only a vast collection of isolated objects and facts, on closer observation is found to be pervaded and permeated with a deep and far-reaching philosophy; and as at first it increases our knowledge it also at length disciplines the intellect into a higher style of thought. So, too, in respect to the more spiritual exercises and attainments, our sense-perceptions are our earliest instructors. The world is full of beauty, of which, however, only the few whose eyes have been opened have any adequate notion, while the moral intuitions challenge attention as veritable phenomena, which, however, prove effective or otherwise in proportion as they become objects of earnest and interested attention. The first great lesson in practical education is how to observe, which, of course, requires the quickening and the proper direction of the perceptive faculty; and the range of actual observation must be as broad as the mind's possibilities.

The stores accumulated by the sense-perceptions constitute the raw materials of which the superstructure of learning must be built up, and with which the processes of all educational development must be conducted. It may be conceded, as we are often reminded, that learning and education are not identical, and that there may be much of the former where there is comparatively little of the latter. But the converse of that proposition is not to be conceded; for learning—a knowledge of things—is a pre-requisite to a broad and liberal education. Each item of knowledge that enters into the mind has its educating capabilities, and usually a man's culture, as well as his intelligence, holds pretty close relations with his acquaintance with things. Gradgrind's preference for "facts" as the chief element in school instruction was not, therefore, necessarily so absurd or altogether wrong as it is sometimes assumed to be; for these, stored in the memory, need not be like the hoard of the miser, useless and unavailable lumber, but rather they are the elementary substances which, cast in the crucible of the mind, are wrought out into systems of thought which fashion the soul's thinkings and believings, its sentiments and its whole condition.

In this preliminary discussion we have purposely only very incidentally and briefly referred to that which must constitute the principal feature of what must be further considered by us—the religious element in education. We have done this in order, first of all, that the subject of education in all its breadth may be clearly in mind before passing to a single department, though that may be altogether the most important. It is necessary, however, in viewing the untaught mind upon which the processes of education are to be wrought, and while indicating the faculties and susceptibilities to be dealt with, to recognize that element in man's original nature by virtue of which he may become the subject of religious instruction. That man is, in the depths of his nature, a religious being, is attested by the entire history of the race and by the practices and institutions of mankind in all ages and countries, and in all states and conditions of society. Among the unconscious intuitions of childhood, antedating the earliest logical exercises, is the sense of duty, with the discrimination of right and wrong in both conduct and character; and this the riper thinking of later years confirms and intensifies. And although these ideas and sentiments are evidently quite independent both of the senses and the reasoning powers it is certain that no others are accompanied by clearer convictions of their essential truthfulness. In philosophical language this is named the ethical element in the human character; in its relations to men's activities in their social relations it is styled the moral; and when considered in its relations to the supreme object of its devotion, whose being it intuitively apprehends, we call it the religious. By virtue of this element in human nature, with its active instincts, the conscious soul not only confesses the claims of duty but delights to respond to them, and it feels the uplifting of its aspirations in worship. And yet, although he is the subject of these intuitions and spiritual susceptibilities and aspirations, still every man comes into the world without the knowledge of the only proper Object of devotion, of whom indeed he can have no adequate conception except as he is taught. And in this fact is seen the supreme necessity and importance of specifically religious education.

The child, at his awakening to self-consciousness, detects the ethical elements in his own nature, and instinctively defers to it as the supreme law of life; and over against this stands the parent, who is to the child in God's stead. The "commandment with promise," which enjoins reverence and obedience to one's father and mother, standing in the sacred decalogue between those that relate directly to God alone and those which impose only social duties, seems to imply that the required obedience is of

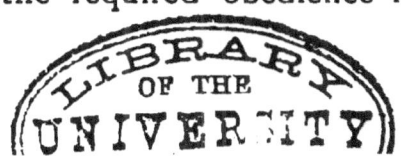

the nature of piety. And the frequent and emphatic references to it in the Scriptures seem to assume that filial obedience, or the lack of it, indicates and hastens the tendency of the child toward goodness of character and devotion of life, or toward sin and impiety. By this divine order the home, with its hallowed associations, is constituted the primary school, the infant-class, and the "kindergarten," in which, according to God's appointment, each one receives his first lessons both in science and religion; and for this there can be no adequate substitute. And when the child has outgrown his childhood, and a wider field with more varied lessons has become necessary, the school succeeds to the parent's place, often indeed performing some of its chief duties very inadequately, but needing to maintain, as far as possible, the authority and the persuasive power of the household. To render this service, at once so important and so difficult, is the special office of our Christian schools. And may we not say, without fear of contradiction, that just here we stand among the appliances and conditions for the performance of these duties?

We have now attempted to bring before our minds the receptive subject upon which the processes of education are to be wrought out—mind at first without knowledge, yet gifted with large susceptibilities, and surely growing up to demand instruction and to receive its permanent character by means of its education and discipline. We have labored to show that the complete, the ideal man, must excel in knowledge, in taste, and in virtue, and that practically to realize this character is the great end of Christian education. At another time we will consider more definitely its character and conditions.

II.

CHRISTIAN EDUCATION—ITS CHARACTER AND CAPABILITIES.

IN our former lecture, which was designed to be only introductory, we endeavored to bring clearly into view the rational human subject in his formative state as the person upon whom the work of practical education is to be performed. We designed in it to give, though briefly and succinctly, a somewhat comprehensive survey and enumeration of his natural capabilities and conditions, by virtue of which an ideal human character might be brought into view. We are now to proceed to a more circumscribed field of inquiry, confining ourselves, for the purpose of greater definiteness of thought and expression, to the capabilities of the mind upon which a specifically Christian education is to be wrought, together with some of the conditions and agencies among which that work must be done. Here we shall have occasion to devote especial attention to the religious possibilities of human nature, of which we said only a very little in what we before noticed; and while recognizing it as the most significant part of our general subject yet reserving its fuller and more adequate discussion for the present time. To that part of our subject we come now to devote the present hour.

We have definitely recognized the religious element as an original attribute of the human nature, and assumed that it is distinctively the property in man that renders him capable of being submitted to the processes of a religious education; we come now to consider more in detail the requirements, the methods, and the results of those processes in their practical operations. We have seen that the religious instincts of the soul make themselves felt at a very early stage of the life of the subject; they are also among the strongest and most persistent. They project themselves into the life unasked, and they persistently refuse to be repressed. They are found about equally effective among all classes and conditions of men; the savage and the sage are alike subject to them. They belong about equally to all the periods of the life-time. They manifest their presence before the dawning of reason, and in all after life they are chief factors in shaping the character and actions. They impress the nascent intelligence with the ideas of right and wrong; and as they reveal themselves without having been learned they are clearly of the nature of intuitions. And out of these arise by the simplest and most direct suggestions the notions of duty and responsibility ; and because they impel the soul to worship, and to blindly reach out after a suitable object to which its devotions may be rendered, and as the mental vision becomes cleared, they postulate God, the infinite, possessing the essential attributes of personality.

As with all other intuitions, these are original and ultimate, and they are not subject to the reason except as their reality is recognized ; for they can neither be proved nor doubted, and they are also indestructible. Their teachings may indeed be temporarily overborne and obscured by the force of the natural appetites and passions ; but they will come again and assert their place in the consciousness. If left uncared for and uninformed they readily lead to superstition, and in that form degrade the soul to spiritual baseness and lead it to ruinous subjections through debasing forms of worship. If, on the other hand, they are resisted, and their resultant impulses suppressed, the whole soul is dwarfed and deformed, and afterward they return again as tormentors.

The first impulse of the religious instinct in man is to worship; and this impulse continues operating with undiminished force in all the subsequent stages of normal spiritual growth. But why it should worship it neither asks nor answers, for it is not the business of the instincts to offer reasons for their own being. Nor is it, as is often the case with the instincts, self-directed to its appropriate object. It therefore demands instruction. But if the one supreme and only fitting Object of devotion is not found, the worship, which cannot be restrained, will be given to some inferior Object-creature of the imagination —idols, fetiches—which the fancy clothes with some of the attributes of divinity; and as is the object of worship so is the spiritual estate. A base object of devotion debases the character that is devoted to it.

The connection of morality with religion is neither an intuition nor is it the result of any direct instinctive tendency of the mind. In most religious systems the ethical element seems indeed to be entirely wanting. No worse crimes have ever been committed than those that have been perpetrated in the name of religion; and no lower depths of moral degradation have ever been reached than have been seen in connection with specifically religious observances. As flagrant illustrations may be named the worship of Bacchus and of Venus among the cultivated Greeks, the murderous rites of the Thugs of India, the *auto-da-fés* of the Romanists, and the "blood atonements" of the Mormons. It is therefore the peculiar and distinguishing honor of the

Christian religion that it makes the purest morality, an ideal exaltation of the ethically good, an important and essential element of its substance. And in this is seen the indispensable necessity for religious education, in order both to direct the soul's aspirations to the essentially good, and to clothe the dictates of righteousness with all the solemn authority that is intuitively ascribed to the accepted object of worship. Men need to be taught whom they should worship, what are the attributes that distinguish him, and by what authority he demands that we should be like him in character and life. And in response to this want the God of the Bible has revealed to us both his person and his law; the one to stand forth as the embodiment of all spiritual and moral excellence and the other to dictate our actions, and the two acting together to constitute the best possible provision for religious culture and discipline.

Conceding, therefore, as we must, the need of a revelation directly from God, and accepting the holy Scriptures in that character, we find in them our sole and all-sufficient guide and instructor in respect to both devotion and duty. Of course it is no part of our purpose, at this point, to set forth the evidences of Christianity, nor to defend the authority of the Bible; for although these things be matters the discussion of which may not be evaded, yet in our present inquiry they must be assumed, for the religious education that we are now advocating is specifically Christian, and our Christianity is that of the Bible.

In the development and growth of man's nature the religious element comes forward side by side with the animal instincts and psychological tendencies; which latter, though not incompatible with the largest increase of the former, are not in harmony with the requirements of Christianity, which not only claims a place in the mind for the religious instincts, but also demands that these, properly instructed and divinely regenerated, shall dominate the will and govern the whole life. The demand made by Christianity for the complete and exclusive control of its subjects, including at once the thoughts and intents of the heart and the conduct of the life, arrays against it all the selfish impulses and tendencies of the " natural man; " and yet in this exclusiveness is its strength. To obtain and to hold this supreme ascendency of the spiritual over the carnal, the religious over the selfish, is the end of self-discipline, to aid in which is among the best offices of Christian education.

The instinct to worship makes two important requirements, obedience to which calls for large subjective readjustments, amounting to a real and thorough transformation of the character. It demands that its object shall combine as personal attributes all ideal excellence; and so it indicates in advance what must be the attributes of its divinity. This, it is true, is often seen only very dimly, and not sufficiently clearly to guide the soul to the apprehension of the truth, and especially so since the moral intuitions are limited in their action by spiritual depravity. And yet these dark feelings after the truth instinctively proceed in the right direction, and intuitively recognize its object when found. No other object of worship than the God of the Bible can answer to the instinctive cravings of the soul; and yet, although God's holiness is approved by the conscience, still the dominant impulses of the natural man are not in harmony with either his attributes or his commandments.

And yet this instinct confesses, and indeed requires, that its object should be in every thing supreme, and that the heart and the life should be subjected to it. But over against this stands the man's own will, claiming the supremacy. Thus there is found a schism, a disharmony in the soul, which as life progresses inevitably grows into an active hostility: "the flesh lusteth against the Spirit, and the Spirit against the flesh, and these are contrary the one to the other." And since the demands of the conscience are imperative, and may not be compromised, their preference above all others is a pre-requisite to the soul's peace. This enthronement of the spiritual over the sensuous and natural in man is designated in Holy Scripture, "being born again;" in theological terminology it is called "regeneration;" but we are now to speak of it as the outcome of the education of the spiritual man. This work, as to its outward aspects, begins with the reception of spiritual truth by the understanding, when it at once demonstrates its quickening power; for "the entering in of God's word bringeth light," and shows the conscious soul its own needs. It also displays its authority, and commands obedience both of character and of life. Christian discipleship is a pre-requisite to Christian education, which becomes effectual only under the "yoke" of Christ, borne and worked in, which is the divinely designated method of learning of him, and of coming into that state of spiritual harmony that there shall be "rest to the soul." This dominance of the depraved self-will is called, in the language of the schools, "depravity;" legally, it is "rebellion;" ethically and spiritually, and as related to the divine Law-giver, it is sin.

In nearly all practical education the negative processes are scarcely less important than the positive; and especially in religious education to unlearn is no less needful than to acquire new thoughts and better methods of thinking. New habitudes of mind and heart, a reconstruction of the spiritual self, are the conditions, both prevenient and subsequent, of effective Christian education.

Passing now, in our inquiries, from the inward and subjective side of our theme to the outward and practical, we may next ask what are the methods and agencies by which the contemplated work may be accomplished? As to the source of the matter to be taught, and also largely for the method of teaching, we turn with all confidence to the Bible as containing an incomparable system of truth and duty. It alone reveals to the rational soul the spiritual world, the supernatural cosmos, in whose atmosphere the supersensuous man lives, and moves, and has his being. The things there manifested, though they belong also to the natural understanding, and largely enhance its stores, more directly address themselves to the spiritual nature, both to instruct and to transform; and yet they may become comparatively ineffective through neglect or misuse. This fatal tendency to rob the truth of its legitimate power, perhaps to change it to a lie, demands especially the counteracting influences of Christian education, and personally of Christian instructors. The lessons by which the expanding mind is to be edified in the truth, and the footsteps of ingenuous but unwary youth are to be guided to the paths of wisdom, must be drawn from the sacred treasury of truth and wisdom. And here, especially, is the practical wisdom of the Christian educator called for, to give to each his portion in due season, milk or strong meat, as the subject shall be able or have need, and every thing administered with the skill of one not a novice.

A special excellence of the Bible as an educating agency is the peculiarly human form in which its lessons come to us. It is quite possible that truth, however abstractly presented, would prove practically valuable, but much less so than when set forth in concrete forms. In the Bible, however, more than almost anywhere else, the highest and the essentially spiritual truths appear humanized and incarnated; and it was evidently the design in the bestowment of these sacred realities that they should be cherished in the heart's deepest affections and given out from warm and earnest souls. Only the smaller part of the influence of the religious instructor comes direct from the truths he declares; his highest effectiveness goes out from him unpurposed, and his best lessons' are those which enter unconsciously into the mind and heart of the learner. An all-pervading atmosphere of truth and goodness is the necessary and the surely effective condition of religious instruction. It is this that so often makes even the humblest Christian home the most successful of Christian seminaries; and as far as possible (and beyond what point is it not possible?) the same atmosphere should be reproduced and rendered permanently effective in all our Christian schools and colleges. It is a sad thought, too often realized, that our Christian youth, who have been nurtured in homes of piety, when removed to our nominally religious seminaries have found themselves in a widely different spiritual atmosphere, and exposed to many hitherto unknown temptations without compensating safeguards. Our Christian homes, with their unworldliness, are the sheltering frames in which the tender plants are kept secure from the blasts of sin till the heart becomes strong in truth and goodness. But if too soon removed, and if their new environments prove uncongenial, how many such must perish miserably! These are thoughts to which the most earnest consideration should be given, with corresponding practical efforts by the founders, curators, and instructors of all Christian schools. It is of small account, if the institution is only nominally and formally Christian, that its founders were professedly Christian, and that it is patronized by an ecclesiastical body, unless its whole spirit and purpose shall be distinctively, and somewhat intensitively, religious.

It is not an altogether uncalled-for suggestion to say that a school founded and carried on by an evangelical Christian denomination should be, in fact as well as in name, a religious institution. The conventual schools of earlier times (and of the present also) embodied the important idea that the Church should be a patron of learning, and that the education given to the youth of the Church should be Christian education. Some of the features of those religious institutions may still be detected in the traditions of our colleges; but it is to be feared that about all that was distinctively religious in them has been eliminated or permitted to perish. It may be well that all fanatical and ascetic practices have ceased, with all sourness and affectation of piety; but it is not well that instead of these our nominally religious schools should be given up to intellectual godlessness and negative impiety. True religiousness is neither ascetic nor fanatical, but healthful, breezy, and robust, while, also, it is earnestly devout and delighting to worship. And yet even this religious state will not come about of itself, and among the many adverse tendencies that are in the world, and from which the best Christian communities are not exempt, only the most earnest and the best adapted religious culture can effectually counteract the almost universal tendency to backsliding.

There are also peculiar liabilities to spiritual remissness in some of the conditions of student life. Any change from the home-life, with its sacred associations and its conservative conditions, is necessarily not entirely free from peril; and these may be largely increased according to external circumstances or personal characteristics. With even the least perversely inclined the mind's occupation with its daily studies, and its engrossment by its round of duties, may crowd out other and better things, and leave neither opportunity nor inclination for the special exercises upon which the soul's health is dependent. The rapid transition through which the mind of the student is passing, with the attainment of new intellectual conceptions and the increase of purely secular knowledge, render necessary corresponding increments of spiritual knowledge to counteract the mind's tendency to drift away from spiritual thoughts and associations, and so to lose their saving power. Many a Christian student who would have been horrified at the thought of backsliding, has been surprised by discovering that, while engaged in his proper studies, all unawares he had declined in spirituality; that the light in his soul had become dim, the ground had slipped from under his feet, his first love had grown cold, and that, while successfully prosecuting his outward duties, he had insensibly, but disastrously, fallen away spiritually. These peculiar temptations and dangers of student life should especially engage the thoughts of those who are charged with the duties, not only of secular teachers, but also of religious and spiritual guardians and guides; and only as these spiritual wants are provided for and imparted by them can the action of the Church be justified in devoting its means and energies to the founding and sustaining of schools and colleges.

The moral and religious training of large bodies of students associated in communities is to a great degree mutual and co-operative. Every such community has its own prevailing public opinion, its peculiar ethical code, and its recognized, though unformulated, laws of living. These may possibly be Christian, wholesome, and salutary; but there is a perilous possibility that they will be quite otherwise. At no other point in the administration of the affairs of such communities of young persons is there so much need of godly wisdom, the very best qualities of head and heart conjoined, so as at once to command and persuade. And here the wise administrator will practically confess that in order to command he must first persuade; and he will also know that while the heart of youth may stubbornly resent the blows of authority it is as plastic as clay or wax in the hands of the skillful molder. Students are as largely endowed as other persons with the usual elements of human nature, and the ordinary laws of Christian morality apply to them as fully as to others; and to these the Christian instructor may always safely appeal. And to such an appeal every right-minded body of students will cheerfully respond, and will fashion their ethical code and public opinion accordingly. And that this may be so, those who have the care of the manners and morals, and of the spiritual life of masses of young persons should see to it that their own personal relations to those over whom they would exert a saving influence are both intimate and effective. To repress and restrain wrong tendencies in associated bodies of young people by authority may be difficult or impossible; but at the same time to lead out their minds, and inspire them with better thoughts and purposes, may be easily practicable. This is among the high functions of the religious educator.

As a state of mental increase and enrichment is the normal condition of student life, so should the minds of the learners be drawn out into higher and broader ranges of religious thinking. The child thinks as a child; but when grown to intellectual manhood the childish thinkings, however excellent for their time, must be put away. To provide for this transition, which is sure to come, a correspondingly broader range of religious discussions and instructions must be brought into requisition. Christian ideas must be carried into every department of thought into which the minds of the learners are led out, and the spirit and the truth of religion must be made to permeate the whole cyclopedia of learning. In those wider ranges of thought unsolved questions and unresolved doubts will often arise, which the habit of independent thinking to which we train our young people may render all the more perplexing and dangerous. Into these mazes and seeming contradictions the teacher must accompany his pupils, clearly recognizing them as such; solving all reasonable doubts, and restraining undue speculativeness respecting the many and great moral and religious problems which lie beyond the range of intellectual knowledge; for there are bounds beyond which finite intelligence may not proceed, and to know these is excellent knowledge, and to practically confess them a high style of wisdom.

The basis of personal faith changes with the

changed conceptions of things which occur, in a greater or less degree, in the history of every individual; and these are unavoidably attended with peril. A man's notions respecting spiritual things at threescore are not the same that he entertained in childhood and youth; and the extent of these transitions is greatest with those who make the largest advances in knowledge and cultured thinking. The faith of the child is pure and simple, accepting whatever is declared by competent authority, and in the absence of other knowledge it is not troubled with any apparent difficulties or contradictions. But with riper years come also broader views, which suggest many and very perplexing questions; and these, if they relate to things that may be known, must be satisfactorily solved, or else they will become occasions of established doubtings, marring the symmetry of the faith of the soul and removing it from its steadfastness. Could one live and die among conditions that effectually separate him from the possibility of any considerable mental growth the faith of childhood might be perpetuated; but not in its simplicity and purity, since the mind's own activities would inevitably store the imagination with a multitude of gross and debasing superstitions. It is not, therefore, without some show of reason that the Church of Rome disapproves of the unlimited diffusion of religious knowledge among the unlearned, holding that learning genders doubts and heresies, while "ignorance is the mother of devotion." But the faith that subsists because of ignorance is itself feeble and unsteady, and the devotion that it promotes is not that "pure worship" by which God is glorified and the soul of the devotee enriched. The position of Protestantism in respect to this matter is the extreme opposite of that of Romanism; and, because it holds that true Christian knowledge is both the promoter and the guardian of saving faith, and a sure source of robust and wholesome Christian character, it claims for every man the privilege and the duty to know for himself what are the great and essential truths of religion, which every Christian should know as of the essence of his creed, and which he is bound to believe to the saving of his soul. And as we would have all men know the truth because we believe it to be incomparably preferable to a form of faith that outrages the understanding and dwarfs the spiritual being, so we are also aware that the darkness of ignorance which engendered the sickly devotions of the cloister and the confessional, the worship of pictures and crucifixes, and which demands the surrender of one's soul with unquestioning subjection to the will of a man, has, as to ourselves and among the conditions in which we live, become forever impossible. As we would not, if we could, have the common people untaught in the truths of religion, so we could not, if we would, remand them to ignorance of the truth and a condition of intellectual and spiritual slavery. We must, therefore, accept the conditions imposed by the free thought of the people, with its consequent labors and perils.

Education, unless it embodies a large and broad religious element, tends inevitably to skepticism. If the individual has in himself, by virtue of his Christian life and the Spirit's testimony to the reality of spiritual things, a constantly assured faith, he will be able successfully to overcome such temptations to unbelief. But such cases, though happily not rare, must be considered as exceptional; and therefore every student should be considered as needing to be perpetually grounded anew in the faith. Any system of education, therefore, that is not clearly and distinctively religious is dangerous to the Christian stability and the moral characters of the learners. Religion must be kept steadily in view in every department of instruction; not merely a philosophical naturalism and a conventional morality, but the system of truth and doctrine of which God is the source and center, Christ the revealer and apostle, and the Bible the heaven-given depository. And this system must be presented, not as something that must be blindly accepted in deference to its authority, but with accompanying proofs and evidences which shall effectually counterwork the mind's natural tendency to unbelief. Glorious and venerable as are the truths of Christianity, and powerful as it is to demonstrate its divinity to the spiritual consciousness of all who have received its truth in the love of it, it is still needful to demonstrate its credibility by reasons addressed to the natural understanding. The teacher having removed, as certainly he will, the pupil's traditional form and foundation of religious beliefs, is now bound to build him up on other and better evidences.

That we may impress these thoughts the more deeply, we reiterate them, even at the risk of seeming to repeat ourselves.

The Christian educator should be profoundly impressed with the conviction and consciousness that he is leading his pupils through a stage of mental development that is peculiarly full of perils. In childhood we believe what we are taught, and the religious intuitions respond approvingly to the lessons of spiritual instruction, and we believe, not because we have been convinced by arguments, but on the authority of our teachers. And this unquestioning faith continues through life, wherever there is real teachableness, and where also the wider excursions of thought do not come in to demand the reasons for the things that are to be believed. The undeveloped understanding, if accompanied by a devout heart, may be satisfied with the heart's assurance of the truths of religion; but in the absence of such a religious experience there usually occurs with the unlearned a blind and stupid negation of faith, while the better educated find their natural unbelief formulating its objections into systems of positive doubts. Educated minds demand, as they have the right to do, a rational basis for whatever is to be believed. Here, however, is the point of danger in the mental and spiritual history of all who make the transition state from infantile dependence to individual freedom of thought; and here, too, not a few disastrous shipwrecks of faith and a good conscience have taken place, and this especially among the abler students in our colleges.

This significant and momentous truth must, therefore, be confronted and provided for. Education, it should be known, except it has a decided infusion of specifically Christian elements, tends directly and with fatal certainty toward skepticism, and to beget a spirit of destructive questionings respecting all that pertains to supernatural religion; and therefore any system of education is of dangerous tendency that does not so present the basis of the Christian evidences as to answer to the natural and not unreasonable questionings of cultivated minds which have been removed away from the implicit faith of their childhood.

The natural relations of instructors and learners imply, on the side of the former, a thorough and comprehensive acquaintance with the subjects to be handled, with their conditions and relations, and with these is conjoined the authority that is legitimately derived from mental superiority and from the official positions of accepted teachers. And on the side of the learners are confidence in the superior wisdom of those who teach and deference toward their opinions; but also, and beyond these, personal independence of thought must be recognized, and the just demand that for every utterance of doctrine or opinion a reason shall be given. We may confidingly trust that not a few of those who sit at these fountains of learning have other and better forms of Christian evidences than can be given by man to man; but that may not be presumed in respect to all; and even where it is found it needs to be continually supplemented and reenforced by external evidences, especially with those whose habits of thinking are logical as well as intuitional, whose *subjective* faiths require the concurrence of *objective* reasonableness in the things propounded.

Remitting any consideration of the evidences of Christianity, which, however, should be formally presented and elaborated in the curriculum of collegiate education, we may glance for a moment at certain incidental forms of proofs that are suggested by the religious intuitions themselves. The soul's impulse to worship requires for its legitimate use an object upon which it may be exercised; and therefore—agreeably to the obvious and apparently universal law, that an original want implies the existence of that which may answer to its demands—that impulse authorizes the presumption of the existence of some one possessing in his own person all the natural and moral perfections which the soul instinctively requires in the object of its devotions. And to this demand no other *one*, real or ideal, except the God of the Bible, the Christian's God, makes even an approximation to a satisfactory response. There are "gods many and lords many;" but no one of these measures up to the soul's intuitive ideal of the object of its admiring devotion, and therefore the thoughtful worshiper turns away from these abortive begettings of the imagination, darkly feeling after the Unsearchable, and asks for something better, and perhaps in his blindness he sets up his altar, "To the Unknown God," assuming that God is, but is to him unknown. The Apostle's announcement on Mars' Hill is of universal acceptation; that which the heart instinctively demands, the unknown object of its untaught worship, is clearly revealed in the Scriptures. The whole world—the universe of thought, say the wise ones—is made up of correspondences, of pairs, each one of whose members implies the existence of the other. There is light for the eye, and sounds for the ear, and hardness for the touch; there are order, beauty, and sublimity that answer to the æsthetical requirements of man's nature; and so there are infinite power, wisdom, and goodness embodied as essential attributes of the God of the Bible; and in him the soul's instincts to worship find all their requirements met with absolute fullness. This form of Christian evidence, while it may be appreciated by the least cultivated, loses none of its power in the clearest light and the furthest reach of cultured thought, and to its impressiveness even the least spiritually-minded cannot be entirely insensible. This "coigne of vantage" should be occupied and turned to account by the Christian educator; the heart wants its God—will worship him if found. It is his duty to guide the inquiring spirit to that which it seeks.

These natural wants of the soul reproduce themselves in forms modified according to their changed conditions in human society, that more comprehensive individual sometimes called humanity. It craves to be organized, is miserable till that is affected, and yet its constituent elements, left to their own perverseness, seem to be incapable of coming into a harmonious unity. The individual cannot attain to any thing at all worthy of his own possibilities except in co-operation with others; and yet as seen in his natural estate every man's hand seems to be against his fellow. War appears to be the normal condition of the race, and accordingly the same word may designate with equal fitness a stranger and an enemy. But Christianity, by mollifying the natural savagery of the individual and by infusing into the soul an all-comprehending spirit of divine charity—so changes the spiritual polarity of the social elements that man tends instinctively to his fellow-man; and the mass, hitherto disintegrated and inharmonious, now, by the impulses of each heart, readily crystallizes into a beautiful and harmonious unity. For this the social philosopher has no alternate or substitute; and because man is by his natural instincts, and by all the requirements of his nature, a social being, Christianity is the first necessity for his temporal welfare. A state of facts so obvious and so suggestive ought not to be neglected by the Christian educator, both on account of their relations to the Christian evidences and their practicable availability in adapting men to the high duties and relations of the Commonwealth. In every department of the social and political sciences, as well as in the more abstract philosophy of the intellect and the heart, there is need of the specifically Christian element. It is, indeed, present both as a fact in the world's history and as an effective factor among the working forces of society. Its recognition, and the illustration of its methods and its effectiveness, and the inculcation of its spirit, should therefore constitute a primary element in the lessons announced from these professional chairs. As the great end of education is to render its subjects capable at once of the highest personal excellence and to make them the best possibly adapted to promote the social welfare, and as these qualifications result the most surely and effectively from the Christian element in education, it is plain that any system of instruction is excellent or defective in proportion to the presence or absence of the Christian element. The injunction of the Master, "Learn of me," has a much wider application than to personal religious life.

III.

CHRISTIAN EDUCATION—ITS PURPOSE—THE WHAT-FOR OF EDUCATION.

CONCEDING the desirableness of education—which, indeed, all our conditions take for granted—it is pertinent that we should ask, What is its purpose and in what consists its value? To this question we may answer in the words of a living writer of high renown—Mr. Herbert Spencer—though we would give to his words a much broader application than he does. He tells us, " To prepare us for complete living is the function which education has to discharge." We accept this statement as both comprehensive and felicitous, and also as well adapted to suggest both the object to be pursued in practical education and the methods of doing the work. But we should not confine our considerations to merely secular affairs, as Mr. Spencer's unspiritual philosophy compelled him to do; but seeing in our broader outlook other than merely secular relations, which qualify and vastly elevate our conception of " complete living," we must comprehend in the measure and scope of the things to be cared for in education all that relates to the spiritual life; and as we claim that these are incomparably the greatest of our interests, and that "complete living" is especially concerned in them, we must also contend that the spiritual character of its subject is the chief concern in practical education.

Our notions as to what education is for and what it is designed to accomplish for its subjects, will largely determine both its substance and its methods. These we have already indicated as consisting in the proper development and discipline of all that belongs to man's real nature; and manifestly, therefore, the neglect of any part of his essential manhood must result in an unsymmetrical and unwholesome condition of the mind and character. Education is neither designed to extirpate nor to suppress any of the elements of human nature originally given by the Creator, but to afford to each due opportunities and helps for their full and proportionate increase. And yet, while all these should be duly cared for, still, since some are more excellent than others, more immediately vital and practically valuable, these should have the preference, and the others in their proper order should be subordinated. This is according to the infallible teachings of holy Scripture, which recognizes all our wants and provides for their supply, but for each in the order of their excellence. The inhibitions of some things, while others are enjoined, must be understood in many cases as relative rather than absolute, as when we are taught to "take no thought for the body," or "for the morrow," but instead, to seek first "the kingdom of heaven."

It is especially needful that in our conceptions of the subject we should be guarded against the perils of a merely sensuous worldliness, caring only for the material and secular, to which there is so often an undue tendency; and nowhere else is this caution more needful than in practical education.

Men are not often better than their own ideals in either life or character. In that fact, and the causes which lie back of it, is seen the great value of noble and worthy conceptions of one's possibilities and the desirableness of lofty aspirations. The original purpose of every creature is indicated by his constitution and capabilities, and even his felt wants and instinctive hungerings and thirstings are prophecies of what may be realized. Each one, also, who rises above the lowest sensuousness in his wants has his ruling purposes, toward the achievement of which he directs his efforts, and in the success of which he rejoices. But it often happens that this success most clearly demonstrates the emptiness and insufficiency of the things that are earnestly coveted; and accordingly the lament of "the

Preacher," who spoke also as the wisest of men and the wealthiest of monarchs, "Vanity of vanities, all is vanity," has been the common refrain of those who have reviewed a career of merely worldly success, while spiritual things were disregarded.

But in order to give a practical direction to our thoughts we will now consider some of the purposes of education as they are viewed among men. The lowest, and also the most prevalent, is that of a merely personal secularism, in the estimation of which education seems valuable chiefly as the means of gaining a livelihood. This, in the language of its own school, is the "bread-and-butter" argument. Nor are we disposed to altogether despise even this. It may be conceded that if education only helps its subject the better to provide for his physical wants it does a good work, though surely not its best. The irrational brutes have their natural wants, and in the order of nature and by means of their untaught instincts God cares for them. But for man, who is a rational soul, made in the image of God, to be shut up within these conditions surely cannot be accounted "complete living." And still it may be granted that the skilled mechanic is better than the unskilled laborer, who is also better than the untaught savage; the engineer is more than the fireman or coal-heaver; the artisan whose deft hand is the instrument of a disciplined mind is of more account than he whose life is only a manifestation of brute force directed by his untaught will. The learned professional—the counselor and orator—are better paid, and worthily so, than the multitude of the unlearned about them; but even in their cases their superiority is chiefly in the incidental results of their better mental training. It is quite evident that in the struggle for existence, which is so fiercely contested in civilized society, the educated have very considerable advantages over the uneducated; and, therefore, were there no higher motives, that fact would suffice in favor of giving the advantages of education to as many as possible.

There is cause to fear, however, that this, the lowest and the least worthy purpose of education, may be made the ruling one, and so the character and kind of the education desired may be unfavorably affected by it. All this, indeed, is much more than an indistinct apprehension of a possible evil; it is already upon us, and its presence is felt in all our schools, from the lowest to the highest. The careful parent, provident of the secular welfare of his children, sees in their education the best assurance of their success in life; and young persons looking out into the future think they see in that direction the most promising prospects; and so education is chosen as the best assurance of simply material success. This, perhaps, should not be denounced as positively bad; it is, indeed, relatively better than brutish unculture and savage improvidence; but the motive is unelevated, and the results in those who are swayed by it must be comparatively disastrous.

Our whole system of public education is just now assailed with a loud and imperious demand in favor of such changes in the course of instruction that (in the language of the complainants) education shall be more "practical;" and by this is meant, that education shall be so ordered that it shall become more surely and immediately available for making money or securing pecuniary interests. And accordingly our highest institutions of learning, the oldest and the most renowned colleges and universities in the country, are modifying their course of study in favor of "technical" education, with necessarily corresponding disfavor toward those that tend, first of all, toward culture—that which shall educate the whole man, and especially the higher and more spiritual elements of his character, instead of those that remove him in the least degree from merely mechanical forces and the operations of dumb animals and inanimate machines. We ask, on the contrary, that the instruction to be given in our schools shall aim to develop and fashion lofty intellectual and spiritual character, with knowledge and appreciation of things that lie beyond the range of the senses— that is, the true, the beautiful, and the good—rather than the most complete machines the more effectually to minister to the grosser wants of men's natures. Our objection to thus secularizing education, and compelling it, like blind Samson, to grind in the mill, is not only that it is a diversion from a higher to a lower purpose, but, still more, that it is a prostitution of the noblest capabilities to gross and corrupting uses. Productive industry is a necessity, and, properly managed, tends to public and private welfare; but unless subordinated by a strong will to other and higher interests it readily becomes an evil of no ordinary proportions. Its ideal is an unelevated one, and it necessarily leads to correspondingly unelevated pursuits and associations. The cultured mind craves a better portion than any thing that can be entered in the merchant's ledger or disposed of by devise; a treasure even for present use that moth and rust cannot corrupt, nor thieves take away. There is indeed a "wisdom" whose "merchandise is better than that of silver, and the gain thereof than fine gold," to obtain and retain which is the purpose of education; and of that design it is capable if it shall be faithfully directed to it. And shall an agency of such noble capabilities be desecrated to the grosser forms of material acquisitions? To live only in order to devote one's energies to money-making certainly is not "complete living." Men's better natural sentiments unite their protests with those of religion against the desecration.

A less gross and materialistic purpose for which education may be sought, if not higher in the scale of morality, is to increase its possessor's ability to serve himself; for men have learned the practical wisdom of the maxim, "If thou doest well by thyself all men will speak well of thee." Because of its power to elevate the character and to increase the mental resources of its subjects, and to give men influence among their fellows, the ambitious and self-seeking may very naturally desire to avail themselves of the benefits of education. Of the greatness of the advantages, in respect to these things, of thorough mental training there can be no question. In nearly every possible position in life the educated man has the advantage over the uneducated, and in many places—and these the most influential and remunerative—only the educated can enter, or, having gained a place, can either respond to its claims or utilize its opportunities. The shrewd and wisely-calculating parent, seeing these things, chooses that his son shall be educated, that he may thus be the better prepared to engage in life's battles and the more certainly assured of success. And the young man, inflamed with a high ambition for public honors in any of the great walks of life where honors may be won, wisely seeks the aids of education for the furtherance of his purposes. And perhaps we are justified in presuming that this consideration, more than any other, serves to replenish our institutions with their annual recruits of students, and those, too, of the better class. The prudent parent or guardian, knowing how readily "riches make to themselves wings and fly away," and that education is inalienable and enduring, and always available, seeks it as the best and surest provision for those whose welfare he would promote. And the thoughtful young man looking forward to active life, and inspired with a laudable ambition to turns its opportunities to account, wisely judges that his surest way to success is to fit himself for life's conflicts by this most promising preparation. Nor are these considerations to be condemned indiscriminately, but rather are they, in themselves, to be applauded, though the final estimate of them must depend upon the uses to which the advantages of education shall be devoted. If the chief purpose is fame—to gain the praise of men—if the attainment and the maintenance of one's social position is the ruling motive, the purpose, though not the lowest, is still much below the proper elevation; and while its pursuit is attended with peculiar difficulties, its highest possible success is sure to bring disappointments. This, too, may be inspired by a narrow selfishness; for the advantages of education may be desired not for generous and philanthropic uses, but for self-aggrandizement. How far these defective sentiments may have operated toward crowding these halls with expectant multitudes of generous youths we need not inquire too closely. If any have so come, it is the business of their instructors to show them a more excellent way. The ruling idea in that case is success in the conflicts of life, with the possible awards of wealth and honor and power among men—a prize altogether unspiritual, and appreciated chiefly by men's lower nature—while it lacks adaptation to the soul's higher and better aspirations. It is also a preparation for a conflict in which only a very few can succeed; and with them *it does not pay*.

Still another not inconsiderable, though still an altogether inadequate claim, why education should be valued and pursued, and one, too, of which much account is often made, is its power to minister to some of the higher wants of its subjects. Education, combining intelligence and culture, adds to one's powers to enjoy, and so increases his internal resources, and also provides for their gratification. There is sometimes a kind of indolent contentment which subsists with only the least help from either knowledge or culture, but the plane of such a life is a humble one, and its pleasures are low and unsatisfactory. The poets and idealists tell us of the delights of Arcadian simplicity, the guileless pleasures of peasants and shepherds, whom they transform into nymphs and swains; but all these are simply ideal pictures whose models are not found in the real world. Wordsworth's "Simple Peter," a man, indeed, but the least possible removed from the brute, is a much more real and truthful image. "That the soul be without knowledge is not good," is not only a divine revelation but equally a lesson of human experience. The mind instinctively craves instruction, just as the physical system craves food; and if in either case the needed supply is withheld, disease and dwarfings and malformations will be the result. Education brings to its subjects larger capabilities for elevated enjoyments, and so diverts the heart's interests from whatever is merely sensuous, and therefore degrading. As weeds spring up spontaneously and grow without cultivation, but bear no valuable fruit, so the grosser elements of human nature develop themselves without being cultivated, but can give but little real pleasure; while whatever is truly excellent must be planted by instruction and cultivated by discipline. The facts of society abundantly confirm these things. The notion that uneducated peoples, nations, or individuals are exceptionally pure and innocent is well known to be quite the opposite of the real state of the case, as may be abundantly proved by observation.

In the absence of culture the lower elements vitiate the whole nature. Depravity of character and viciousness of life, which necessarily result from the lack of education, entail innumerable discomforts; and these, in the case of the uneducated, are rendered the less tolerable by the absence of the spiritual resources which invariably accompany mental culture. Popular ignorance is never separated from social and domestic wretchedness; and had it no higher functions, the promotion of education would be sufficiently justified by its beneficent social influences. And what is true of communities is still more so in respect to individuals, to whom education becomes a constant resource for pleasurable living.

Among the notable advantages of education to the individual is the ability that it gives him to derive pleasure from all his surroundings. From his cottage on the hill-side the man of cultured sensibilities derives larger values from Cleon's broad acres than are all the stores that they yield to their owner's garners. Leaving out of the account for the moment all properly religious considerations, but remembering, meanwhile, that they must finally determine the case in its completed results, it will still appear very clearly that the man of the world, the genuine epicurean, must crave for himself the benefits of education, in order that he may revel in his mental resources and hold high converse with his own thoughts, and with other minds, living or departed, with whom he may associate.

To such a one nature becomes a vast gymnasium, well stored with the means of giving pleasure, while art brings her ministries of painting and sculpture, of architecture and landscape gardening, and of the melodies and harmonies of song or the moving voice of oratory. To him every sense, and also the stores of a cultivated memory and the beautiful creations of a vivid imagination minister the loftiest thoughts upon the noblest themes, and all his spiritual resources contribute to his pleasure. Evidently, therefore, even in respect to only the present world and the things that pertain to it, education may claim no inconsiderable place, appealing to men's self-love in view of its ability to contribute to their temporal happiness.

But from the higher, the specifically Christian point of view, all such estimates of life are not only " incomplete," but positively and fatally defective in respect to all that is noblest and best in "living," and that, too, as to the things that belong to the present world. Only as men live for others do they attain to " complete living," while the man of the world lives only for himself, or, if he seeks companionships, his ruling motives are still his own pleasures. His highest thoughts stop short of the realm of the spiritual and ethical, and find their sphere, at the very best, in the æsthetical in taste, and not the conscience, making pleasure, and not duty, supreme.

Nor need it be denied that in all this there is a real joy, and that the character so brought into view may possess many admirable qualities; but its defects and positive faults are also very great and manifest. Intellect and taste are worthy to be praised, but the conscience—the moral element in the soul—transcends all else, both in its intrinsic worth and in its relation to men's happiness. And yet it may occur that while the former two may be liberally educated and broadly cultured this latter may remain uncared for and inadequately developed.

And where this is the case there can be neither symmetry of character nor "complete living." Every man owes back to society all that he has received from it, according to his ability, and his selfish devotion of all that he has to his own pleasing is a fraud against humanity that will inevitably return to vex him.

These considerations have led some whose souls were raised above such cultured epicureanism, but not quite up to the Christian standard of entire consecration, to include in their inventory of right living an ideal and practical philanthropy; the service of the State and humanity. The religious element in man's nature, separated from its supreme object, often expresses itself in admirable forms of philanthropy and patriotism and in acts of heroic and unselfish devotion, which the world is ever ready to applaud. An illustration of this is seen in the legend of Curtius's throwing himself into the chasm in the forum, that so it might be closed, and also in the more authentic story of Regulus. We see this in the philanthropy of a Girard or Peter Cooper and the noble deeds of our "good Samaritans;" for, though godliness is never developed from man's nature, a kind of natural goodness is still possible, and education may evoke this. It displayed itself in the lofty ethical system of the Stoics, and it is seen equally clearly in the delicate and sturdy sense of honor sometimes manifested even by savages. But as these things result from instincts rather than from culture—perhaps often from direct divine inspirations—and they appear alike in the learned and the unlearned, though no doubt culture favors their development, they lie outside of the definite limits of our present discussions.

The glory of man is, that he is not like other denizens of our world. In strength, in agility, and in beauty, these are his rivals, and often his superiors; while over against his reason lie their instincts, which, if less various in their adaptations, are much surer in both their coming and their uses. In contrast with his irrational competitors, and in respect to simply mundane affairs, there is certainly not much reason why the wise man should glory in his wisdom, or the strong man in his strength, or the rich man in his riches. Man's superiority must be recognized as consisting in that by which he is contra-distinguished from all other creatures: his spiritual nature in its purely religious and its ethical intuitions and capabilities. And because of its transcendent excellence this element of his character should be especially cared for in his education, in respect to both right being and "complete living." As, therefore, "the Christian is the highest style of man," not the religious sentimentalist merely, nor the trained theologian, who believes, but not "with a heart unto righteousness," so should education in its purposes and methods be directed especially to those things through which Christian character and Christian living may be infallibly secured. How this may be done must be clearly apprehended before the work can be entered upon with any promise of success, and for that purpose right notions of the character to be acted upon must be entertained. And here it is found that before instruction can do its best work there is need of a radical and thorough rectification of the spirit. That "man is very far gone from original (essential) righteousness, and in his own (proper) nature inclined to evil," is not primarily a theological dogma, nor wholly a truth of revelation. It is a matter of fact patent to all observers and confessed by all real philosophers of the mind, who concede that in order to its needed elevation a regenerating process must take place in the character. But by what agency this radical transformation of the character is to be effected the philosophers do not inform us. The ablest of them confess that it is (and from the nature of the case must be) a mystery. The ultimate processes by which character is transformed lie deeper to the soul than the farthest reaches of the consciousness. We know the results, but neither the effectuating cause nor the manner of its proceeding. It is also philosophically manifest that the power that shall fundamentally transform the interior nature must originate and operate from a source beyond the subject acted upon. To change the course of nature requires a force outside of and superior to nature. This idea is one with which the readers of the New Testament are familiar. The divine Teacher spoke of it as a "being born from above," and an apostle amplifies this thought by predicating of saved souls a spiritual renewal; a "being born again, not of corruptible seed, but of incorruptible, by the word of God, which liveth and abideth forever." From the side of philosophy comes the response—it is in Coleridge's words—"I utterly disclaim the notion that any human intelligence, with whatever power it might manifest itself, is alone adequate to the office of restoring health to the will ;" but he continues to say, in substance, in a dependent alliance with the All-perfect and Supreme Reason, of course, changing the original basis of action, the human will may be effectually harmonized with the divine. And here again even our philosophical guides bring us back to lessons of sacred wisdom. " The fear of the Lord "—a devout subjection of the human to the divine will—" is the beginning," the formative element and condition, "of wisdom." With this, which by nature we have not and cannot obtain, all correct education of the spiritual man must begin.

In the presence of a body of Christian educators and students these things may seem to be only truisms, which all recognize and accept. Be it so; but their value, and the possibility that they may be lost sight of, much more than justifies this reference to them. It is not that specifically Christian instruction is out of place or entirely unavailing before the regeneration of the spiritual nature is completed, but that its success in fashioning the character requires that process as an attending condition; and to it also all real Christian teaching tends. And only by virtue of the new spirit received in that process can the proper ideal of moral excellence of character be even approximately realized or the conduct be raised to the standard of "complete living." But this spiritual regeneration, because of its subjective nature and its influence upon the moral elements of the soul rather than the intellectual, is neither education itself nor the direct agency for that work, though it greatly facilitates it as a predisposing cause. But every thing is still to be learned, and the renewed habitudes of the spiritual man are to be confirmed and hardened into enduring consistency. Intellectual and spiritual growth proceed most symmetrically and successfully, and each ministers to the increase of the other while proceeding side by side; the head and the heart in harmony.

The notion that has so widely prevailed, that there is a necessary antagonism between secular and sacred learning, and that there is an incompatibility between the scholarly and the Christian characters, results from viewing the subject from a wrong standpoint. The same God is the maker of both the head and heart, and he is "not the author of confusion, but of peace;" of harmony not less among the powers of the mind than in the Church. The healthy development of the mind requires that with the increase of secular knowledge there shall be a like growth in the knowledge of things spiritual; that the quickened conscience and enlarged moral susceptibilities shall be illuminated by the light of the understanding and directed in their outgoings by knowledge and a sound judgment. God has joined them together in order that each may minister to the other; and that, growing up together, both may realize their highest possibilities. The mind that goes forth in the domains of nature searching for the truth, if accompanied and possessed by the spirit of faith, finds in every thing the demonstration of

God, in his person and his works, his creatorship and his providence. If the intellect is educated and the moral nature dwarfed there will result unbelief, and the negation of faith, pride of opinion, and inordinate self-consciousness; and if, on the other hand, the religious sentiments are disproportionately developed alongside of a barren waste of thought, there is always a liability to superstition and dangerous fanaticism, to instability and the possibility of being led into hurtful and destructive errors. "Complete living" is, therefore, the result of complete education, both of the head and heart, the intellect and the emotions, the understanding, the sensibilities and the will, the logical, the æsthetical, and the ethical elements of the man, the judgment, the taste, and the conscience. Let all these be equally educated, and each enlarged according to its capabilities, and the concordant principles of truth, beauty, and goodness wrought into the substance and fiber of the character; then "complete living" will cease to be a shadowy ideal—to be seen dimly in the unapproachable distance—but it will have become a realized fact in the soul's spontaneous action. And since the correct ordering of the life and character is to be effected in opposition to the strong impulses of the lower elements of men's natures, with their inborn depravity, the stronger force of objective authority is needful to overcome these and to enthrone the conscience over the renewed will. Perception of the right is not alone sufficient to insure its observance; beyond and above this must be the sense of duty to deter from the wrong and to impel to the right the disciplinary force of Christian instruction.

We have yet two subsidiary thoughts to be considered before passing from this part of our general subject:

First, That the adaptation of Christianity to man's nature emphasizes the utility of specifically Christian education. We have attempted to show, from the natural constitution of man, that in order to his highest culture a prominent place must be given to moral and religious instruction and discipline. If now we reverse the process, and approach the subject from the side of practice and experience, the same conclusions are reached and still more directly enforced. The domination of the appetites and passions is a painful and degrading slavery, and their service is both a weariness and a dwarfing of the soul. And if, rising above these merely animal desires, the dominion is given to "the lusts of the eye and the pride of life," there will still remain unsatisfied longings, and the noblest aspirations of the soul will be held in check. Even with the widest learning and the most appreciated culture "the eye is not satisfied with seeing nor the ear filled with hearing;" the starved and defrauded spiritual nature still reveals its presence, and the soul's unrest demands its vindication. Only as the moral nature is developed by education, side by side with the other and less spiritual elements of the character, can its better possibilities be realized and the harmonious action of the powers of the soul secured.

Our second thought, with which we will close, is that since education very greatly enhances the capabilities of its subjects, there is a corresponding need that these increased powers should be tempered and directed by correct moral influences. The voice of warning against the perils of "godless schools" is not a false alarm; the danger is real and may be very great. And accordingly the Church has, at all times, wisely concerned itself with the work of education, not only in respect to specifically Christian doctrines and duties, but also in all that tends to mental growth and the fashioning of men's characters. And it should not be forgotten that mental growth without a corresponding development of the moral nature tends fatally toward spiritual depravation and enmity against God. It is, then, quite possible that our schools, our whole system of secular education, shall become seminaries of speculative and practical ungodliness. The Church, therefore, acts only in response to an imperative requirement in founding and maintaining institutions for the promotion of sound learning, for the needful education of its youth among the salutary and hallowing influences of religion, and to give due effect to that purpose it devolves upon those who are charged with these sacred interests the high duty of making the teaching specifically and emphatically Christian. Surely a Methodist school should be, first of all, religious.

IV.

LIONS IN THE WAY—SPECIAL PERILS AND HOW TO TREAT THEM.

THE author of the Book of Proverbs presents in the form of a parable the cowardly and self-excusing plea with which "the slothful man" seeks to excuse his remissness, "There is a lion without, I shall be slain in the streets." The fact declared might be true enough; but the fault was, that it was used as an excuse for cowardly indolence, and not as an incentive to earnest duty. The lesson of the proverb is, that though there be difficulties and dangers in the path of duty, only "the slothful" will for that reason hesitate to walk in that way, with the additional intimation that only to such are the difficulties insurmountable or the dangers especially formidable. The author of the *Pilgrim's Progress* weaves both the imagery and the lesson of this proverb into his narrative, with suitable amplifications and embellishments. There were lions, he tells us, one on either side of the narrow way; so that in attempting to avoid either there was a liability to come too near to the other, and each seemed to be waiting for his prey. But in fact they were chained, and at so short a tether that the pilgrim could pass safely between them. So, though they were real lions, and therefore dangerous, they could not harm him so long as he used courage and discretion.

Almost every enterprise has its difficulties, which the "slothful" may readily magnify into lions; and in all human affairs failure is a contingent possibility which must be avoided by wise and brave action. In the things connected with Christian education there is a full share of these contingencies, which the wise and conscientious instructor will recognize and duly appreciate. Such is human nature, and such are the influences among which personal character must be fashioned, that its moral elevation requires conflict in the process, so giving to its successful accomplishment the character of a victory. The natural difficulties of the case, also, are greatly intensified in the conditions of young persons actively and rapidly increasing in knowledge. Some of these, which are inseparable from the conditions of mental growth and development, we have already sufficiently indicated. We have now to consider some which belong more specifically to the present times and the prevailing conditions of thought. The thinking of the age is steadily changing its points of observation, and so obtaining new and broader and more correct views of things; and these changed views necessitate new adjustments of thought respecting some things closely related to the truths of religion. These changes cannot be avoided; we think, too, that they are desirable; but they impose upon the Christian educators of our times a sacred and somewhat difficult duty.

During the present century very great advances have been made in nearly all departments of human learning, of which progress the broader and better methods of thinking that have come into use were at first a procuring cause, and it was afterward intensified by them. These advances of learning have been made especially in the domains of the natural sciences and of biblical criticism; and in both parts they have impinged upon some traditional and time-honored opinions concerning religion. Until comparatively lately, on account of the lack of secular learning among the common people, religious teaching, based upon the English Bible, had the undisputed right of way, and the methods of using the Bible were also, in many things, sadly defective in style and form. But all this is now changed; another authority has come into the council, demanding to be heard in the arbitrament of learned questions, and accordingly the whole system of religious beliefs must now be adjusted to these changed conditions. The Bible is no less an authority than before; but another authority has come into the court, and the claims of both parties must be heard, and harmonized by the needed modifications and the just partition and distribution of the domains of each. To the Bible must be conceded the supreme authority in all things spiritual, and those directly relating to men's relations to God and to the kingdom of God in the earth and to the future state. But in whatever relates to material things nature must be allowed to speak through its facts, and men must hear. The first principles, the elements of physical science, are found in the material world, and its conclusions are to be derived from these and not from the Bible, which surely is not a text-book of natural philosophy; nor should it be compelled to stand as an authority in geology, or physics, or psychology. The processes by which natural and spiritual knowledge in their severalty are attained are essentially diverse, and each kind is independent of the other, and, therefore, each should be shut up to its own specialties. The two books—nature and revelation—are both of God, and they are, therefore, alike infallibly true, and each is supreme in its own domain, and because they proceed from the one eternal fountain of truth they cannot contradict each other, though to men's limited observations their teaching may sometimes seem to be irreconcilable.

It is also becoming more and more manifest to our wisest and most devout Christian thinkers that the Bible is largely an undeveloped mine of spiritual treasures; that hitherto the Church and Christian thinkers have navigated only the shallows and the narrow friths of its boundless ocean of spiritual mysteries, which the divine Spirit is appointed to make manifest in due time—and this thought should teach all men to hesitate before announcing as a finality their own partial conceptions as the complement of what the Bible teaches. And as to men's knowledge of the material world, it is in respect to phenomena scarcely more than infinitesimal in comparison with what is still unknown; and as to an all-comprehending and combining *rationale* of the material universe, the most learned scientists have not yet mastered its alphabet. It is therefore quite too soon for the contestants respecting the teachings of revelation and the findings of science to make out a definite inventory of their distinctive claims. Whatever the Bible clearly declares, and of that there is very much that is both indubitably manifest and unspeakably valuable, we gladly accept and appropriate. But just what may be the relations of these spiritual realities to the world of matter and of the natural laws among which we live may not be entirely manifest. So, too, natural phenomena, which fall within the range of the sense-perceptions, must be accepted as reliable data of knowledge; and still further, carefully drawn inferences and rigidly scrutinized generalizations must also be accepted for the time being, and until further knowledge shall require their modification or re-adjustment. But it is the temerity of ignorance to set up these half-understood phenomena and their still more shadowy suggestions against the truths of revelation, and, also, because our knowledge of the Bible is quite the opposite of infallible, they who attempt to interpret its lessons should not be too dogmatical. Some things have certainly been learned from both nature and revelation, but very much more remains to be learned; and in these unexplored regions there may still lie concealed some of the great factors that make up the problem of being.

For its own purpose—namely, our religious instruction—the Bible must be accepted as a divinely-given embodiment of truth and doctrine, and even its references to natural things are subordinate and auxiliary to the same purpose. In respect to these things its point of view commands the apparent and phenomenal rather than the occult and unknowable reality. As a record designed for all ages and conditions of mental growth no other form would have been suitable; for a revelation, that it may come within the sphere of men's knowledge and so become a manifestation of the truth, must appear in the setting of their conceptions. And yet those materialistic conceptions are not an integral part of the truth which they invest. To those to whom the words of revelation were first given, the earth appeared to be a flat surface, walled in by the horizon and canopied by the sky; and the truths of God delivered to men with such conceptions necessarily entered into the same conditions. And when the ideas of other worlds came to men's minds these were assigned positions indicated by their character, above and beneath. All this was manifestly the result of the mental preconceptions of those to whom the revelation was made, and they indicate not the real but the phenomenal world.

The practical problems thus propounded are not peculiar to this age, and the best minds of Christendom have all along so understood the language and imagery of the Bible; and as required to do so, by the growth of physical science, they have made haste to modify their conceptions of the sense of the text agreeably to the better knowledge of the material things of which it incidentally treats. But the rulers of the Church have not always been equally wise, as was seen in the case of Galileo; and our own time has produced its full share of the same kind of folly. It was certainly wise to interpret the language and imagery of the Bible just as they appear till it became manifest that such a course must involve absurdities; for old and prescriptive notions should not be lightly abandoned. A plea in mitigation may therefore be offered in favor of those who opposed the Copernican system as a dangerous heresy; and the same consideration should be extended to the many good people who in our day are alarmed at the teachings of the natural sciences. So while we respect their cautiousness, and excuse their ignorance, we cannot be expected out of respect for them to deny manifest truth. This unreadiness of those who are not experts in science to accept the vaticinations of the professed prophets of nature, is also somewhat justified by the overweening pretentiousness of not a few smatterers in science, who have attempted to build up great theories on very narrow bases and with scant materials, and also doing this in a spirit of intense and unreasonable opposition to the truth of the Bible.

If we are really believers in the truths of Christianity, assuredly for us there is nothing to fear in respect to the stability and perpetuity of the great system of spiritual truth of which the Bible is the embodiment and depository; and they do but little honor to the faith which they would cherish and protect, who are alarmed at every threat against it and dread to see it submitted to the severest tests. The aphorism uttered by Macaulay respecting the using of the Baconian philosophy, that it calls for much hope and very little faith, is especially needed to guide our modern scientists: the former to quicken their researches, and the latter to save them from the characteristic folly of their class, of shouting Eureka before any demonstration has been reached. The great truths of religion are much more than merely traditions; for they have demonstrated their vitality and power through the ages; and they are therefore not to be lightly set aside, and especially not in obedience to the requirements of systems that seem to be as unsteady and evanescent as the shifting lights of the aurora borealis. And yet it would indicate a combination of fanaticism and stupidity to refuse to accept the well-established results of science for fear that the faith would suffer loss. Christianity is not a house built on the sand, and needing to be guarded by ecclesiastical canons and fortified by ignorance; but it is built upon the Rock, and stands secure. No truth has any thing to fear as to the outcome of any fairly-conducted examination of its evidences; and the mistaking friends of the Gospel who deprecate such discussions do it a disservice. And yet, because the unlearned and unskillful are liable to be moved from their steadfastness by superficial and specious arguments, it is needful that they shall be protected by their teachers with better instructions. This is the sacred and the delicate duty of the Christian instructor—to lead his pupils to better conceptions of the truths as they rise out of their childhood's unreasoning faith into broader and clearer perceptions. And just along this path are the "lions" at which the faint-hearted are alarmed, and which without proper guidance may prove fatally destructive. But, like those of the *Pilgrim's Progress*, these lions are harmless if dealt with boldly and circumspectly. To deny or ignore all these occasions of harm would be to act like the proverbial ostrich, that when pursued hides her head in the sand and fancies there is no danger because none is seen. There are indeed dangers that may not be disregarded in the things of which we have spoken; dangers that should be recognized and confronted boldly and wisely; and if so dealt with they will prove to be as harmless as the chained lions. But to attempt to evade the conflict is to insure defeat.

The questions arising out of the learning of the times and affecting the evidences of Christianity are of two kinds: those that relate to the natural sciences, especially geology and biology, and those that are developed by biblical criticism. And these are practically the more formidable on account of the spirit of skepticism that pervades and animates much of the learned criticism of the age, and the illogical audacity with which conclusions are proclaimed before the conflict of arguments has been fairly joined. It may be conceded that the results of scientific investigation and of critical inquiry have very considerably changed the external aspects of the conflict for and against the Christian faith. New questions have been raised, which, unanswered, would soon become fatal objections; and these are known not only to every scholar, but effectively to every one, old and young, learned and unlearned. Our church schools teach the sciences that are being used as engines for the overthrow of the faith; and whoever studies the Bible in our Sunday-schools is reminded that the genuineness and the integrity of nearly all the sacred book have been called in question. These are the issues that are forced upon all Christian teachers, whether in the pulpit or in the professor's chair; and to the latter pre-eminently belongs the duty of engaging in the strife, which is perilous only as it is neglected. Let us then, as we proceed, consider these several subjects as they seem to relate to the things that are taught us out of the Bible.

Geology, the science of the earth viewed as dead matter, is, as a science, scarcely a hundred years old, though both the sacred and the profane literature of all ages contain geological facts and references. As a science it is also still in its infancy, with but few of its problems fully resolved, and of the thousands of questions suggested by its ascertained facts only the smallest part have been satisfactorily answered. Still some things have been clearly made out, and some important principles have been determined, which only the folly of ignorance will attempt to belittle. And some of these have pretty close and effective relations to certain things found in the Bible, which have also been wrought into theology and become integral parts of the popular faith; and to adjust these things satisfactorily, and to harmonize the two sets of truth, demands close and intelligent consideration. And it may also be said they have compelled the adoption of modified views of some things in the Old Testament history and of biblical interpretation generally.

One of the early battles of geological science against the traditional interpretation of the Bible was over the six days of creation as found in the beginning of Genesis; and this has resulted, it must be confessed, in the thorough defeat of the traditional method. We have ceased to hold and teach on this subject as we did fifty years ago, when our best biblical scholars insisted that the only possible meaning of the "six days" was six periods of twenty-four hours each, with their dawns and twilights; while to-day no scholar will so declare. And yet this wide change has not harmed our confidence in the Bible. That patent fact is assuring in respect to some other things not yet so clearly concluded, involving, among other subjects, important questions relative to the Old Testament Christology, and to the place of man in the creation; all of which questions will no doubt find satisfactory solutions as they arise and are duly examined. The now generally accepted notion of the indefinite extent of the period designated "six days," during which our earth was passing from chaos into a state adapted to human habitation, sweeps away a multitude of otherwise very formidable difficulties, and especially so some of those connected with the scientifically-attested fact that man is evidently the latest found of the earth's denizens. While allow-ing any required length of time for the pre-Adamite earth, the testimony of the rocks and of the gravel-beds, the caves and the estuaries, calls for no greater age for the human race than is easily reconcilable with the allowably rectified chronology of the Bible. The whole difficulty that has seemed to arise from the evident antiquity of the earth is thus at once and effectually disposed of, for in the chronicles of the ages of the Almighty millions of millenniums cost no more than single years. Through these apparent mazes and over these necessary transitions of views and opinions our Christian instructors are called to conduct their pupils, and to demonstrate to them the essential harmony of all that is really known of science and revelation.

The study of biology, with its related matters, opens a wide field for inquiry, which is as yet only very partially explored, though here too some highly important facts and principles have been definitely settled. We are here also brought into contact with not a few important questions that are more or less closely related to biblical and theological subjects; and they, therefore, call for intelligent and judicious treatment by our Christian educators. In this examination Nature appears as an independent witness to give her testimony upon subjects in respect to which the Bible has also spoken. These witnesses are independent, each of the other, and both are alike credible, for neither of them can be untrue ; nor is it allowable to suspect that they can contradict each the other. In considering these things it is, first of all, necessary to ascertain just what the Bible declares about them, and also to carefully consider what has been clearly proved respecting the phenomena of living things. The first result of this process would be a not inconsiderable abatement of pretensions on both sides in respect to the extent of our knowledge and the infallible correctness of the conclusions that have seemed to be reached ; and the next result would be, that since these things are viewed from diverse points of observation by these two witnesses, it may be reasonably inferred that what may seem to be contradictory is so only in appearance, and that fuller knowledge would disclose the most complete harmony.

It is quite possible—may we not say it is very certain ?—that in matters relating to natural science more has been inferred from the language of the Bible than can be legitimately justified ; and it is unquestionable that many things announced by the scientists with all the apparent authority of oracles, are often simply hypotheses, or at best only theories, in the construction of which a very large part of the materials have been contributed by the imagination rather than gathered from well-ascertained facts. To place these things in their true relations is a delicate and a needed work, demanding alike spiritual illumination, large acquaintance with the phenomena of nature, and thoroughly rational modes of thinking. But until this whole subject has been subjected to the treatment which can only thus be given to it, it is too soon to assume that there is, or can be, any conflict between science and revelation.

A hasty reference to some of the undisputed facts of the physical world may help to a better understanding of this subject. The things of the whole world appear under four different forms:

1. Inorganic matter.
2. Vegetable life.
3. Animal life.
4. Rational life.

All these the materialistic scientists tell us are only different conditions and aspects of matter, and that they shade into each other without any ascertained or probable lines of demarkation between them. It is assumed that what is sometimes called dead matter has in itself the elementary principles of all life, the " potency and prophecy of all phenomena," which are sure to be developed in organic forms, wherever the conditions are favorable. This is the much-talked-of theory of evolution, respecting which very much has been said and written, and with about equal unwisdom on both sides. But the thoughtful scholar, whether a Christian or a skeptic, while he confesses on the one hand that there are facts in nature that may be readily built into such a theory, yet, on the other hand, he must concede that the phenomena of nature are not, as a whole, in harmony with its requirements. The real philosopher will, therefore, suspend his judgment and ask for more light, and the Christian believer, with his "more sure word of prophecy," will abide in his faith and await, without fear or misgivings, all that science may disclose.

The several forms of existence which are seen to stand distinct in their phenomenal aspects, have never been proved to be otherwise than essentially diverse, and incapable of transmutation, under the last analysis to which they have been submitted. Theorists may talk about the unity of nature and the upward gradation of being, without a break or chasm from the lowest to the highest, from the dull clod to the ethereal spirit, but the empiricist has no testimony by which to sustain such a fancy. The chasm between inorganic matter and living organisms has never been bridged, although learned and expert physicists have examined nature " with tortures," in order, if possible, to extort that secret; but in no case has life been evolved by any of the processes of chemistry, and while there is absolutely no direct proof that life has been evolved from what seems to be dead matter, the negative proof is complete and overwhelming that it cannot be done, since as to the facts of nature, organic life, in every known case and among all conditions of being, is seen to be the result and offspring of pre-existing living organisms. So, too, the two forms of living things—vegetables and animals—though apparently scarcely distinct in some of their lowest forms are found on closer inspection, to differ essentially in their characters, and therefore to be incapable of transition the one into the other. Vegetation, in its merest approach toward its ideal perfection, is apparently further removed from animal life than in its lower and less developed forms; and at every point nature seems to declare that the chasm between its two forms of life is absolutely impassable.

In man is seen still another form of life—the spiritual—which cannot be identified with his animal and physical nature; for there is an absolute want of proof that the rational soul is the product of man's physical being, or that the physical instincts lie in the same plane with the reason. And so we find these several forms of existence, each with its proper *differentia*, and with its metes and bounds clearly established, and which cannot be over-passed. And while we may not accept the Bible as a competent authority in the science of biology, we cannot but recognize the remarkable agreement of the story of the creation of the earth, and the herb, and the living thing, and finally of man, with the arrangement and distribution of things in the world.

The theory of evolution, much talked of and but little understood, is, so far as it has any scientific basis, shut up to the various forms of vegetable and animal life. It certainly cannot be applied to inorganic matter, which is without growth, and it has never been shown to apply to spiritual beings. Growth is a universal fact throughout the domains of vegetable and animal life, not only as each individual thing advances from its earliest infantile status to its completion, but also that among favorable conditions the offspring rises to a higher stage of perfection than was reached by the parent. There seems to be for each class and kind of living things, an ideal perfection toward which the whole species is tending by the force of its vital instincts, and toward which each individual advances through its proper stage unless restrained by unpropitious environments. And because of the modifying power of conditions and environments, acting unequally in different directions, two individuals of the same kind may grow out into widely different forms and types; and if to these different types shall be given the name of species, then we have before us the process by which specific differences are originated, which may at length become fixed and transmissible by inheritance.

The question of the evolution of species is, by its conditions, incapable of either proof or disproof. All living forms are propagated and perpetuated agreeably to the original law of like producing like; and yet even that law is found to be somewhat variable, and the lines of descent are often seen to be divergent; but whether or not such divergencies are shut up within definite limitations, with ever active tendencies to return to the original types, cannot be determined, for two sufficient reasons: (1) We have no sufficient knowledge as to the original constitution of species, if such there are, and (2) human life, and that of the race, is too short and human observations too narrow to allow any adequate tests by experiments. On the one hand, nature frequently manifests a tendency toward the production of variations, which at length become fixed and subject to the laws of heredity; but, on the other hand, there is no fairly attested case of the production of a well-defined and clearly differentiated species of either plants or animals. Evolutionists account for this lack of proof by claiming that the time required for effectuating such changes exceeds all human calculations, and that during such unmeasured cycles the earth has existed as a seat of life. But the history of those remote ages is written, though very imperfectly, in the form of organic remains in the earth's frame-work of rocks; and that record fails to sustain the theory that the course of life has been steadily and uniformly upward. At the utmost the question is still an open one.

This question of evolution has been discussed with an earnestness that seemed to claim, on the one hand, and to concede, on the other, that its triumph would be fatal to the Christian faith. But just why any Christian theist should be afraid of it is not altogether obvious. The fact that there is method in the processes of nature, and that the tendency is upward, ought not to disprove its divine origin nor exclude the Creator from his own handiwork. We know life simply as a mode of existence and a well-directed potency of nature; and yet assuredly it is not itself a property of matter. And since it is not known what life is, nor whence it is derived, its existence suggests that it comes from an unknown and incomprehensible Power, which, because of the attributes revealed in his works, must possess the nature of a person. The created universe has been recognized as revealing its great Original, and the skill manifested in its ordering has been accepted as proof of the divine wisdom; and surely the laws of life are no less wonderful and theistical than are those of the mechanical forces. To detect God in his works, and to demonstrate from them his attributes of power and wisdom and fatherly goodness, has been the recognized business of natural theology; and surely God is not excluded from his works because they are perpetually in action, moving in changeless order toward the perfection of their possibilities. As his providence is seen in the development of God's purposes in society, so are his wisdom and power displayed in the forces of life in the world.

We have purposely assumed the truth and the authority of the Bible in all that has been said, and such will be the case in all that shall follow; for this is not the place to open that question. But certain questions respecting the Bible itself, what it is and how it is to be used, are coming to the front and demanding to be answered. Our young people and the unlearned are aware that modern scholarship has brought into question certain traditional notions respecting the Scriptures—questions that sometimes seem to involve the first principles of the faith; and to these our Christian educators must render satisfactory solutions. We have thought of the Bible as one--a unified embodiment of divine truth--and such no doubt it is; and yet it is a compilation of documents, and that fact involves the question of the canon. The Bible was originally written in languages now dead, and even the copies that are now in existence are not the originals, but transcripts made in later times. It is called the "word of God," and yet it is mournfully human in its composition and as to its external character. It is claimed and conceded to be inspired; but just what is the substance and purport of that claim is itself a subject to be considered. The task imposed by these things upon our Christian educators is all-important, and is in itself beset with not inconsiderable difficulties; and these are just now not a little heightened by the recent and current discussions of these subjects. A lion of rather formidable proportions is here to be confronted.

We claim for every man the free use of the Bible with the right of private interpretation, and that concession carries with it to the receiver the obligation to read and understand the written word, with the resultant responsibilities. If, in the past, these claims have been only partially asserted, and the people have accepted their theology with unquestioning confidence from their teachers, it is quite evident that we are entering upon a new order of things, and that the intelligent but non-professional Christians of the future will demand intelligible answers to all the questions respecting the Bible. A very heavy duty is thus devolved upon the Christian educators of these times. More intelligent conceptions respecting the authority of the Christian Scriptures as sacred writings, and of the quality of their contents, have become a necessary condition for the maintenance of the faith among us; and while the duty resulting from this requirement comes to all who teach, from the nursery to the pulpit and the professor's chair, to the last, beyond all others, is given the needed facilities for dealing with these questions. The unbelief of the age is concentrating its forces against the citadel of the faith, God's written word; and they to whom belongs the duty of defending the faith must meet their antagonists at that point. Many of the older methods of defense are no longer available, the the enemy having carried some of the outposts that lay beyond the walls of the citadel. Some things that have been supposed to belong to the integrity of the faith must probably be abandoned as untenable. The "hay, wood, and stubble" which human infirmity has wrought into the structure of the traditional theology will perish in the fire of the conflict, but the "gold and silver" of spiritual religion, and the "prepared stones" of Christian evidences, will abide in more clearly manifested beauty and strength. Here is a call for heroic treatment; here, perhaps, is some heavy work to be done, which requires large measures of both force and skill. And to whom is this call more directly and authoritatively addressed than to those whom the authorities of the Church have placed at the fountain-heads of instruction—whose business is "to give subtilty to the simple, to the young man knowledge and discretion?" No doubt, in view of these things, "the slothful man" will say, "There is a lion without, I shall be slain in the streets;" but because of the greatness of the peril the demand for courage and fortitude in those charged with the defense of the truth is correspondingly imperative. The final result is not at all doubtful; about that we have no misgivings; our concern is, that it may be achieved the most speedily and effectively, and with the least possible loss of souls; and that it may be so done our Christian instructors must take hold of this matter boldly, ably, wisely, and in the fear of God, assured of the sufficiency of the Gospel against all its adversaries.

V.

CHARACTER-MAKING.

IN another lecture we accepted the statement that "the function of education" is to prepare its subjects for "complete living." We shall not now either withdraw or modify that concession, but we would lay alongside of it another thought which will help to the better understanding of the things to be considered. The phrase "complete living" is evidently intended to be understood in an active sense, relative to doing rather than simply being; to conduct rather than character. And yet it is evident that the former is dependent upon the latter for its stability and effectiveness, and therefore to insure "complete living," attention must be given to the formation of "right character." Every man's life, as a whole, corresponds to his character; for though special resolves and temporary impulses may have their uses and may, indeed, be necessary, be requisites to the reformation of one's manner of life or the improvement of his character, yet in order that these shall be permanently effective of good results they must pass from the nature of simple impulses and voluntary purposes and become fixed and abiding habits.

The scriptural maxim, "Of the abundance of the heart the mouth speaketh," applies equally to all the forms of men's activities, and that fact justifies the further rule of judgment that "the tree is known by its fruit," and, therefore, that in order that the fruit shall be good the tree itself must be good. "Do men gather grapes of thorns, or figs of thistles?" Every man's active life is a truthful index of the ruling qualities of his mind and heart, the things that constitute his character. The purpose of education is, therefore, to awaken and confirm in the soul, so as to constitute its habits, correct and noble thoughts and principles; and wherever these are found, and not elsewhere, there will surely result "complete living." The purpose of the present lecture shall, therefore, be to indicate some of the conditions and characteristics that are found in all those in whom the good work of education has been perfected.

But before proceeding to consider the furniture and endowments of such minds it may be useful to notice certain needful mental habitudes and modes of thought. Intellectual and moral sincerity is at once a very rare quality of mind, and also a condition essential to either right conduct or a correct character. Prejudices are proverbially unjust, and from them their subject himself is usually the greatest sufferer, since they render him incapable of being just in his opinions and sentiments, and, of course, in his conduct also. The effect of such a distortion and disarrangement of the mind is to disturb the processes of reasoning, to obscure the intellectual perceptions, and to darken and pervert the conscience, which almost necessarily involves personal demoralization, and habitually evil ways of thinking and feeling. And because this perverted condition of the soul is very deeply inwrought in human nature as well as very evil in its effects, it calls for the most earnest and also the most delicate and judicious efforts for its complete correction—a task that is second in interest to scarcely any other.

Nearly related to men's prejudices, though essentially not the same, is the peculiar disposition of the mind—both the intellect and the moral nature—called skepticism. It is the fashion of the times to speak very tolerantly, and indeed deferentially, of what men choose to designate "honest doubt," with the implication that usually doubts, especially in respect to matters of religious faith, are honest. Nothing, however, is more certain than that men's disbeliefs, even more than their beliefs, are formed and entertained quite irrespective of any rational proofs.

To believe without due evidence is to accept a condition of mental slavery, which leads to superstition and the debasement of the character; and on the other hand, to refuse to believe when the proof is at hand is not only logically unjust but unphilosophical, and opposed to correct and symmetrical mental development; and when inspired by dislike of the truth it is morally corrupting. Superstition is a misdirection, and often an abuse of the religious element in the human character, but it still continues its subject in his character and relations as a religious being, so perpetuating in him, even if somewhat dwarfed, the noblest attributes of his humanity. Skepticism, on the other hand, in addition to its utter unreasonableness, is thoroughly destructive of all by which the soul becomes allied to moral excellence. It hides God and the spirit-world from the soul, takes away all faith in the future life, with its awards and compensations, and effectually extinguishes hope, except in blind chances and among the happenings of the present life. It reduces virtue to a childish sentiment or else a romantic ideal, without any corresponding reality, and renders morality only a conventionalism without authority, the sport of every one's passions, with only the faintest security for any real excellence of life or character.

Men's actions are, in most cases, determined by

their characters, and not by the direct influences of either their sense of duty or of interest. They act as they feel themselves impelled by their tastes, inclinations, and habits, and each day's conduct is the result of the present ruling element of their characters. But when a spirit of doubt, of unpurposed but effective unbelief which excludes God and his providence, dominates and fashions all these, the character becomes depleted of moral sensibilities, and the conscience is deprived of its ability to discriminate among moral qualities, and of course it is without authority; passion usurps the place of the sense of right and the present pleasure, and lust or ambition becomes the rule of life. Perhaps the man did not deliberately choose his evil ways, but by becoming separated from the needful aids that come only through the religious instincts, which skepticism discredits and destroys, he was left to become the sport and subject of the lower elements of his nature. Here, then, is work for the Christian educators: to see to it that the subjects of their instructions may be saved from the pernicious power of a soul-destroying skepticism by the shaping of their characters to better modes of thinking and believing. The curse denounced upon those that " remove the ancient landmarks," who " call good evil and evil good," who " put light for darkness and darkness for light," subverting the eternal distinctions of right and wrong, and poisoning the streams of virtue at their fountains, falls. not only upon the purposing seducers from virtue, but also upon all whose unconscious spiritual influences lead away from the truth. Here should the Christian educator stand, like Phineas with his censor, to stay the plague.

After these preliminary suggestions in regard to certain evils to be carefully avoided we pass to the more definite consideration of some things that belong to the character of the properly-educated Christian. Here we assign the first place, the convictions that possess the mind, because they lie at the foundation of character; for it is evidently true, both as to the result of the past and the sure presage of the future, that "as a man thinketh in his heart so is he." Though in our speculations we discriminate between the intellectual and the moral faculties, they nevertheless belong to the same undivided mind, and mutually and very largely affect each the other. A man's beliefs enter into his moral and spiritual conditions, and these in turn react effectively upon his convictions. He that would diligently "keep his heart," because "out of it are the issues of life," must also guard against evil thoughts lest the whole mind be led astray by them. Here may be seen both the large possibilities and the great importance of education, the "instruction" of the wise man whose "reproofs are the way of life," the wisdom which is "an ornament of grace" and "a crown of glory." In considering the purposes for which education is to be sought for it is well, therefore, to fix our minds and thoughts upon the convictions, the habitual modes of viewing things, that should be originated and entertained, since they necessarily become the law of the life.

We are, of course, speaking especially, though not exclusively, of convictions that relate to moral and religious truth; for these are especially and yet not exclusively concerned in Christian education. It is, then, first of all and in the highest degree important that clear and definite notions of right and wrong shall be wrought into the understanding and made to possess the whole soul; since the authority of the conscience is conditioned by the clearness of its discriminations, and its perceptive powers are also enlarged by its activities. These things are sufficiently obvious to all who will observe them; but by being disregarded they become obscured so as to escape attention, just as every-where the senses and the mind's perceptions detect only the things to which they are especially directed, and objects are seen or not seen according to the dispositions and purposes of those present with them.

It is not our purpose to speak of the practical processes of education, by which the soul's faculties are to be adapted to their appropriate functions, but rather to consider accomplished results: the fixing in the mind and heart the convictions that these things are abiding realities, that the discriminations made by the quickened conscience are just and true, sacred and all-important entities, never to be left out of the account, but always to be accepted as constant factors in all the problems of life. There is an infinity of properties and relations in and among the things with which we have to do, some of which seem to elude our observation, and others are of not enough value to compensate our inquiries. But it is not so with things now under notice, for the one thing that is valuable and important beyond all else in our mental furniture is the power to discriminate between the right and the wrong; to recognize the authority of the conscience and to realize the obligation to do right; and that the highest possible advantages of these things may be at once fruitful and abiding they must be wrought into the substance and fiber of the soul's being.

The mind's conception of moral qualities and

their distinctions implies a sphere of thought and life other than that of the senses and the natural perceptions. The subjective consciousness of moral entities implies an objective sphere of being in which those things subsist as substantive realities. The properties of which the conscience approves as excellent are not always identical with those that command the approval of the taste. Their rectitude is different in kind from the correctness of material measurements, and besides and above all merely natural notions of rightness or beauty is its mandatory power, which enjoins duty and will not be denied, and to which the conscience assents and confesses the righteousness of the indicated demand. The moral philosophy that fails to recognize any thing beyond the realm of nature is essentially defective, because it leaves out of the account a present and supreme element of the matter in hand. The form of goodness with which man's spiritual nature is chiefly concerned is not a spontaneous production of the mind, but it supposes a higher source, and a transcendent authority, opposition to which is more than an error; it is sin, whose turpitude is proportioned to the sacredness of the Person against whom it offends. These conceptions of essential righteousness, of duty, and of the authority that gives force to the dictates of conscience, must be so wrought into the mind and embedded in the spiritual consciousness so deeply that they shall become abiding and ruling elements of character. And where these things so abide and dominate the active powers of the soul the conduct of the life will correspond with their excellence, and not otherwise.

With these conceptions is also and inseparably associated that of retribution, of compensations, in the form of honors and well-being to the good and of shame and sorrow to the bad. The natural conscience, even when only partially instructed, appears to have an intuitive sense of something of this sort in the ordering of the world's affairs—the idea of a Nemesis pursuing the evil-doer, which, though apparently eluded for a while, is sure at length to overtake the guilty one. We see this in the case when the barbarians, seeing the viper fastening himself on Paul's hand, concluded that evidently he was a murderer, " whom, though he hath escaped the sea, vengeance suffereth not to live." The illustrations of this intuition, though most commonly recognized in the form of vengeance, because the sense of guilt is nearly always present to the natural conscience, include also many and strongly-marked cases of the opposite character. The heart's intuitions and the experience of mankind unite to respond to the teaching of divine truth, that, "Though a sinner do evil a hundred times and his days be prolonged, yet surely it shall be well with them that fear God, which fear before him. But it shall not be well with the wicked, neither shall he prolong his days which are as a shadow; because he feareth not before God." But there is a broad difference between the heathen and the Christian conception of this subject. The Greek tragedy left its Prometheus to suffer the inflictions of the tyrant's power without compensation or redress; but the Hebrew drama, though it sets forth the sufferings of its hero, tells also of his release and his abundant compensations, illustrating "the end of the Lord," and proving that he is "very pitiful and of tender mercy." Upon the undefined and instinctive utterances of the great heart of humanity oppressed with the sense of sin the Scriptures pour a strong and steady light, clearly detecting and distinguishing the right from the wrong, and assuring to each its appropriate recompense, the whole combining in the unchangeable declaration, "There is judgment with the Most High." This all-pervading and fearfully sacred element of the divine government, which is the manifestation of God's essential nature, is much more than a fact or an established order; it is rather the outcome of eternal righteousness abiding in the Godhead, an essential attribute of his divinity manifested in human character and impressing itself on all that pertains to man's destiny. And because it is of God it not only is and must be, but, which is much more, the natural conscience feels that it ought so to be.

There are also the elements of imperishability in all the ethical and spiritual exercises and conditions of man's nature, by virtue of which the whole character is fashioned and the unchanging destiny determined. This tremendous truth, so incomparably important, so divinely sacred, and so far-reaching and abiding in its results, should be deeply embedded in the convictions and ruling sentiments of the mind and heart. The education which fails at this point, whatever else it may accomplish, and by whomsoever it may be given, is not in the true and best sense Christian education.

Christianity, if not an empty and pretentious system of fables, is specifically and eminently a supernatural religion, and, in order to its practical effectiveness, its supernaturalism must be always and every-where recognized. The reality of that other and greater realm lying beyond that of sense and reason must not only be accepted as a fact (conceded, but not much used in our learned inquiries and discussions), but it must also stand forth as the one controlling factor in all of them. The sphere of nature, to which science is shut up, is vastly less than is that of the soul's activities; and when science can proceed no further faith may properly supplement its shortcomings by supplying, as trustworthy data, what science hopelessly calls for and yet confesses to be a felt want. Science finds the world ready-made to its hand, but can give no account of its genesis; while, on the other hand, "by faith we understand that the worlds were framed by the word of God." The very first sentence of the Bible reveals what science could never have demonstrated, and against which it has nothing to offer. The conception of the supernatural standing over and above nature, embracing and permeating it, brings all the phenomena of the natural world out of the chaotic darkness and confusion of atheism and places them in the light and harmony of a divine order. The one great truth of science, infinitely greater than any other because it is the foundation of all, is God; and this belongs to science only as a postulate, which can neither be proved nor rationally called in question. Philosophy demands God in all the infinitude and almightiness of his attributes; the deepest intuitions of the soul recognize his being and the instincts feel after him as "an infant crying in the dark." Created nature bears his faintly expressed lineaments, "the labor of his hands and the impress of his feet." But all these are but the hidings of his power, and God is really known to men only by virtue of the revelations that he has made of himself by supernatural ways, speaking at first "at sundry times and in divers manners by the prophets," and afterward by his Son—"God manifested in the flesh." And as so revealed God is seen in all his works, the upholder and director no less than the Creator of all things, the Father of the spirits of all flesh, the life and the light of men. He is that sole potency of nature in which all things subsist. He directs the planets in their orbits and listens to the cry of the young ravens. He upholds all worlds, and also beautifies the lilies and cares for the dying sparrows, and he says to men, "Ye are much better than many sparrows." The difficulties that beset the doctrine of the divine providence are not found in the things propounded to our rational thinking, but in that subjective spirit of unbelief which is blind to the truth. To be able to see God by an abiding perception of the soul, though in a high and peculiar sense a divine gift, is also the legitimate outcome of well-directed religious culture, rendered with godly fidelity and accepted and treasured up with faith.

The scriptural idea of God, which is the only

proper theism, brings to humanity the boon of immortality and the future life. As the conception of the supernatural delivers the world of sense from its isolated and infinitesimal individuality and presents it as a portion of the unbounded universe, so the notion of God, the Father of eternity, carries with it that of the imperishability of spiritual creatures made in the image of God. Existence, so contemplated, assumes new and inestimably more glorious aspects, and man, as a spiritual being, is raised above the mutations of material things. The misgivings of the psalmist respecting God's care for man, because of his almost immeasurable littleness as compared with the vastness of the heavens, resulted from the temporary earthiness of his estimate of man's character and of his place among God's works; and all these were speedily dispersed by a better and more truthful view of what man is and as known and appreciated by the Creator. The dark shadows that seem to our unspiritual minds to separate life and death, time and eternity, earth and heaven, melt away and vanish in the presence of a steady conception and habitual conviction of spiritual realities, disclosing in its unchangeableness the broader realm of the divine ruler. It is the false science of superficial pretenders that seeks to separate itself from all beyond the range of the senses, and so to find no place for the Creator in the world that he made and now upholds. But, interpreted by the word and the Spirit, "the heavens declare the glory of God and the firmament showeth his handiwork;" and after these come lessons which reveal the divine fatherhood, the grace of Christ, the comforts of the Spirit, and our immortal hopes. And these are the lessons that should be wrought into the minds and hearts of docile and ingenuous young persons, not merely as abstract truisms perfunctorily enunciated, but as vital, spiritual verities, to be grounded in the heart's convictions and fashioned into abiding characteristics.

Christian instruction, if successfully carried forward to its completed purpose, must extend beyond all merely external influences resulting from the contact of mind with mind. The recipient soul must itself come into new and better habits and spiritual consistencies. The virtues which exercise the moral nature must be more than objects of thoughts, of right choices and duties to be done. They must rather become the attributes of the soul; an inwrought and abiding conscientiousness which moves and acts spontaneously, and almost unconsciously, by its own impulses. It is eminently wise to keep our hearts with all diligence, and happy is he who so watches and prays; but more supremely blest are those whose well-instructed souls rest in God always, having overcome the evil one, and now find God's word abiding in them.

On the human side the corrected moral character appears in the form of conscientiousness, a clear perception, and delicate appreciation of social obligations, with a steady purpose to obey all their requirements; on the obverse, the Godward side, it is a habitual religiousness, the sentiment of the soul toward God, with the resultant emotions and exercises. Though these are called by different names, and spoken and thought of as different things, their diversity is only apparent, not real. Some have vainly attempted to construct systems of morality with the religious element eliminated, and others a system of religion made up of ceremonials and emotions without respect to right conduct. The fault of both of these is something worse than separating what God has joined together; it is the tearing asunder and consequent destruction of the essential nature of which both morality and piety are the necessary outgrowths. The right adjustment of man's spiritual being is, no doubt, as to its efficient causation, the work of the Holy Spirit; and yet for its growth and complete development it is largely dependent on human agencies. The plants and trees that cover our fields and adorn our landscapes are indeed the product of the soil, warmed by the sunshine and watered by the dews and rains of heaven; and yet they attain to their completeness only as they are properly cultivated. And in like manner does the soul, though taught and fashioned by the divine spirit, grow into habits of right-doing and of godliness of thoughts and affections, chiefly as it is moved by the words of instruction and by godly examples and by all the appropriate agencies of Christian nurture. Authority may effectually command obedience, and purposed self-discipline may impel to the performance of duty; and as these proceed the whole spiritual nature will be fashioned into conformity with these active and outgoing impulses, so changing these external influences and purposed impulses into the settled habitudes of the spiritual nature. This is Christian character, subjective rectitude of spirit, the ripe fruit of Christian education. Without this fruitage our best efforts, with the best appointed methods and appliances and the most notable results in other things, are still disastrous failures.

The motives that, in the beginning of right living, usually govern men's conduct, are, no doubt, in most cases mixed and imperfect, not wholly unselfish, and often coming short of ideal completeness. But as the instructed spirit rises into clearer light and becomes more affected by purer and simpler spiritual forces the love of the right (simply as such), the approval of the morally excellent, and the admiration of the " beauty of holiness," become the all-engrossing and dominating affections and impulses. And when this is become a completed work right living will become the assured result.

Before leaving the general subject of these discussions, and along the same line of thought, it may be pertinent to consider some of the specifically personal characteristics of the mind in which Christian education has done its work. One's self is, after all, his own nearest and greatest interest—a truth recognized and emphasized both in Scripture and by the soul's highest and purest instincts; and a proper care for one's self is not at all in conflict with any part of moral or religious duty. It is a false asceticism, quite alien to correct thinking, and entirely other than the consecration of ourselves to God and Christ, taught us in the Scriptures, that asks for such a kind and degree of self-abnegation as would disregard those personal qualities and actions which command the approval of the best men and even compel the respect of the ungodly. Vanity may be a foible and pride a fault, and both of these are doubtless among the things from which the perfect man has cleansed himself; but self-respect is very nearly related to all the chief forms of essential right-mindedness; is itself a virtue and the parent or foster-mother of many virtues. The maintenance of a chastened and justly moderated self-appreciation is especially the duty of scholarly and cultured Christians, whose characters and consequent relations in life devolve on them high duties and assign them an excellent mission.

God himself looks with infinite complacency upon the soul that bears his image, inwrought by spiritual culture; and any man that is renewed and beautified by grace may appropriately glory in what has been accomplished in himself and in what he has become. The wise man may not glory in his own wisdom as if it were the highest, nor the mighty man in his strength, nor the rich man in his riches; for all these are unworthy of an immortal, god-like soul; but he may glory that he knows his God, the author of "loving-kindness, judgment, and righteousness in the earth;" and if he duly appreciates the relations into which he is brought and the honor that God has laid upon him he will not fail also to respect himself, and that sentiment will prove to him at once a talisman and a recompense. That a man should feel that he would be dishonored and his better nature affronted by low or unworthy practices is wholesome and elevating in its tendencies.

The condition of character indicated by the word manliness, though not easy to be analyzed or defined, although it is very readily recognized, is inseparable from any right conception of what belongs to the properly-educated Christian; and to develop and fix that quality in the soul should be the special purpose of all Christian education. It implies a just appreciation of the individual simply as a man, irrespective of all accidental conditions, and also good-will toward all men; and beyond all else it sees human character ennobled by the divine favor. It is not simply tender-hearted kindness and charity, (in its lower sense) but a conscientious appreciation of whatever is really or potentially excellent, wherever it may be found, and a corresponding disfavor toward all opposing qualities of narrow selfishness, of unprincipled self-seeking, and pretentious worthlessness. Its complete development and rounded fullness of proportions implies the presence and effective working of a good conscience, thorough devotion to the right, and a consciousness of fellow-feeling with God himself. This condition of character never fails to make itself conspicuous, but without ostentation, in the whole life and conduct of its subjects; and men take knowledge of them and render to them sincere homage as embodiments of true virtue.

This disposition of mind is also the surest and most excellent safeguard against temptations; not only those of the grosser forms, but also the more subtle and, therefore, the more deceptive; not only against "the lusts of the flesh," but equally so against the "lusts of the eye," the æsthetics that outrage ethical purity, and "the pride of life," which exalts itself and disregards all else. The Christian who, according to his well-instructed understanding and rectified conscientiousness, has learned to respect himself in his true character, is doubly protected against the allurements and impulses that would lead him astray, since his quickened and well-instructed moral sense caused him to feel that only the one right way is at all compatible with his position or worthy of his character. To such a one, because of the clearness of his spiritual perceptions, the steadiness of his convictions of right and his conscientious fidelity of purpose, the call of duty, whether to labor or sacrifice, is as the voice of God, to be responded to only by instant and cheerful obedience. Aware that men recognize him in his true character that fact becomes to the true man of honor a perpetual and effective stimulus to a becoming course of life and conduct and to a devout purpose to live for higher than temporal ends.

The sentiment of honor, though sometimes thought of and considered as belonging exclusively to men of the world, is found in its completeness only as the fruit of Christian culture. The honest man of the stoic age, as sketched by Cicero, is indeed an admirable character; but even he is found in the last analysis to lack the essential element of unselfish goodness, as taught in the Sermon on the Mount, and as seen in the ideal Christian. True honor comprises delicacy of sentiment, a manly spirit, a sensitive regard for the rights of others, which is the only genuine ultraism and supreme moral courage. The slightest touch of any thing base, or mean, or false, or unjust is essentially abhorrent to it, since purity, sincerity, integrity, and truth are its chief ingredients. Nor is it without respect to the good opinions of men, but because of its supreme regard for the right. All such opinions become worthless in proportion to their departure from the standard of true moral excellence. It may cause its subject to be pleased with his influence over other minds and to desire to be regarded with respect and consulted with deference; but it is sensitively jealous of the rights of the lowly and of those who cannot care for themselves. It fully recognizes the appropriate distinctions of social ranks and conditions, giving honor to whom honor is due; but it never forgets that even the most lowly have their rights, and since, because of their own helplessness, such persons cannot protect themselves, the true man of honor, if he has the power, feels himself called to become their champion. This was the chief redeeming element of the so-called chivalry of the Middle Ages, which also appeared in a much better form in the character of Washington. It was seen operating sublimely but madly in the conduct of John Brown, and it was the controlling element of character, of which its subject himself was apparently unaware, that led our martyred President Lincoln always to say or do the right thing at the right time. But all these were but very imperfect approximations to the true ideal, the essentially honorable character, which is seen in fragmentary features in the principles and precepts of the Scriptures, and still more gloriously in the manifestations of the divine attributes, which we contemplate completed in human kind in Him who alone was, in the absolute sense, a perfect man. No better model for an object-lesson, in all that is noble and lofty and honorable in human character, united with all gentleness, brotherly kindness, and purity, can be found or called for than is presented in the character of Jesus Christ.

The Christian educator, therefore, needs this

model, displayed in its simple but sublime truth and beauty, in all his instructions, that its features may be reproduced in the susceptible souls and permanently wrought into the characters of those to whom he ministers. Education becomes Christian just in proportion as the personal Christ is found in it in his truth, his Spirit, and his person.

I have now filled up the time and exhausted the opportunities given me to speak to you upon the deeply interesting theme proposed for our consideration. Only a few of its many points have come under notice, and the discussion of these has been only very general, fragmentary, and incomplete. And yet it may be hoped that even these exercises will not prove altogether fruitless. You will believe me when I say, I place a very high estimate on education and have a profound appreciation of the office and work of the educator ; but these should be definitely Christian in character and spirit. After all, we must come back to God's estimation of these things, " Behold, the fear of the Lord, that is wisdom, and to depart from evil is understanding."

www.ingramcontent.com/pod-product-compliance
Lightning Source LLC
Chambersburg PA
CBHW022136160426
43197CB00009B/1306